150 years of
Doncaster
Plant Works

A pictorial history of Britain's famous Railway Works

by

Peter Tuffrey and Michael Roe

Published

Doncaster 2003

by

Bond Publications and Wabtec Rail Limited

Published: Doncaster 2003

Bond Publications
8 Wrightson Avenue
Warmsworth
Doncaster
South Yorkshire
DN4 9QL

and

Wabtec Rail Limited
PO Box 400
Doncaster Works
Hexthorpe Road
Doncaster
South Yorkshire
DN11SL

ISBN 1-872062-04-0

Printed by Trafford Print (Colour) Ltd, Doncaster and London

150 Years of Doncaster Plant Works

1 The Establishment of Doncaster Works

The Great Northern Railway comes to Doncaster

In the 1840's Doncaster was an elegant market town, home of the wealthy and a major staging post on the Great North Road. This was the era of so-called 'railway mania', with the promotion of a great many schemes for new railways across Britain. Such was the case with influential landowners and businessmen of Lincolnshire and South Yorkshire who in 1844 approached Edmund Beckett Denison of Doncaster, MP for West Riding (Plate 1). Denison was a strong advocate of a direct railway line between London and York. It was largely through his efforts, assisted by local solicitor Robert Baxter that the Great Northern Railway (GNR) was brought to Doncaster. Much to Denison's dismay, the initial plans for the railway routed the main line to York across the fens to Gainsborough and Selby. By August 1844, Denison had successfully argued the case for prominence to be given to a 'Towns' route along the line of the Great North Road rather than the 'Fens' alternative.

Edmund Denison 'Father of GNR'

However, attempts to link the two cities attracted the attention of linen draper George Hudson of York, whose involvement in a number of railway schemes had earned him the title 'Railway King'. It was inevitable that any rival schemes to Hudson's would attract fierce opposition. The 'London and York' Bill, the largest railway undertaking of its time, was laid before the 1845 Parliamentary session. The passage through Parliament was stormy, with much opposition from Hudson's supporters and other vested interests, but finally after many months of legal argument the Bill received Royal Assent on 26th June 1846, and the Great Northern Railway was born. Edmund Denison became Chairman of the GNR in 1847, remaining in office until 1864. His single-

minded tenacity, particularly in the face of Hudson's opposition, earned him the accolade 'Father of the GNR'. The first section of railway was completed in October 1848 with Doncaster joining the GNR network on 4th September 1849. The coming of the railway was to have a major influence on the subsequent growth and development of Doncaster, but as significant was the decision of the GNR in 1851 to build its railway vehicle workshops on the western outskirts of the town.

Peterborough or Doncaster Works?

The Board of the GNR had been largely pre-occupied in the legalities of forming the company, and little thought had been given to where the main railway workshops should be located. In 1848 the GNR constructed its first repair shops at Boston, being geographically central to the company's rail network, but otherwise in a largely rural area. However, the railway had been engaged for some time in lengthy negotiations for the purchase of land at Doncaster, including grazing rights to land owned by the freemen of Doncaster and householders in Balby and Hexthorpe. On 27th March 1850, Archibald Sturrock was appointed as Locomotive Engineer of the Great Northern. In June, an Executive Committee was set up (including the newly appointed Sturrock) to examine various locations for the Works. The group reported back in July recommending Peterborough, which according to Sturrock was 'exactly the distance from London, Doncaster and Great Grimsby to enable your Locomotive Engineer to run engines and enginemen to the most advantage'.

Denison, as Chair of the Board, argued for a delay in the decision and a further Committee was formed in February 1851. They again found in favour of Peterborough, and the report was adopted in May 1851, but further intervention by Denison ensured that the resolution recommending Peterborough was dropped. Finally a proposal was tabled at the June Board meeting 'that Doncaster be selected as the place for the erection for the General Repairing Shop', recognising the town's proximity to large coalfields and iron-founding industries. When the announcement was made in favour of Doncaster the local church bells rang, according to a contemporary report, 'until the wild ear ran giddy with their joy'.

2 Expansion & Development of The Plant

a) 1853 - 1923 Great Northern Railway

Initial Construction Work

By autumn 1851 plans had been prepared by William Cubitt, civil engineer of the GNR, for buildings estimated to cost £45,000. The Company Secretary's office at King's Cross issued an advertisement on 3rd March 1852 inviting tenders for the contract for the repairing shops at Doncaster. On 4th May the GNR Directors awarded the contract to Messrs Arthur and George Holme of Liverpool. This firm would also construct the bridge over the railway to the south of the station to provide access into the Works. The initial building work proceeded in stages, with Cubitt reporting to the Board on its progress. By 24th July 1852 Sturrock had relocated his office sufficiently to Doncaster to address his first letter from the Works. However in January 1853 Cubitt reported that his hope that 'all would be completed by the contract time, 31st March' was over-optimistic.

Cubitt's report of 24th May states 'At Doncaster the work remaining to be done is chiefly fittings and small works of completion the whole is going on very satisfactorily. The building of the fitting shop and offices, the boiler house, the engine erecting shop and smithy and the iron store are complete. Nothing remains to be done except such as office fittings, baths, machine fixing, completing tanks and such matters. The stationary engine will be ready to try in a few days. The steam hammer, two large lathes, the cylinder boring machine and the fans are fixed and the

relatively modest in size and in keeping with the declared GNR policy of overhauling locomotives, but purchasing new engines from outside contractors. The oldest parts of the Works comprise the long building facing Doncaster railway station to the south of the present footbridge, and a number of the workshops located immediately behind (Plate 2).

Within this building (now called Denison House) and beneath the bell tower were the offices for the Locomotive Engineer, his Draughtsmen, Works' Timekeeper and a Waiting Room. Adjoining these to the north were a Committee Room, workmen's baths, a Grinding Shop, Boiler and Engine Rooms, a Store and Works Manager's Office. Over half of the remaining building comprised machine workshops on both floors, named the Upper and Lower Turneries, where line shafting driven from the steam engines provided the necessary power to drive machine tools. The Upper Turnery contained smaller lathes, drilling, slotting and planing machines, including brass machining and finishing areas. The Lower Turnery was equipped with far heavier machines for the turning of axles, and boring of wheel centres and locomotive cylinders. At the northernmost end of the Lower Turnery was a Carriage Shop.

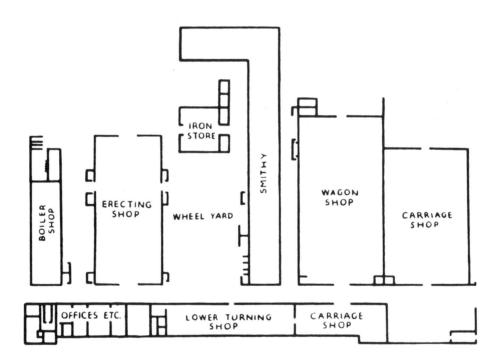

Plate 2 – 1855 Works Plan

foundations of other large machines are in hand.' In June 1853 the blacksmiths were the first group of workers to move from Boston to Doncaster, with the Smithy being the first fully operational workshop. By July, half of the men who were to be transferred from Boston had arrived at Doncaster, and by December 1853 all 700 Boston men were relocated, which along with local labour made up a staff compliment of 949.

The Early Works 1853-1855

The initial phase of building at Doncaster established 5 acres of covered workshops in an 11 acre site,

Behind the bell tower, and set at right angles to it, the locomotive Boiler Shop stood as a separate building. Within the Boiler Shop at its western end were a Coppersmiths' Shop and Brass Foundry, the latter equipped with four crucible hearths. To the north of the Boiler Shop, a yard 52 feet wide was equipped with a traveller to transport boilers to the Erecting Shop. The original Erecting Shop to the north, comprised thirty locomotive berths, fifteen each side of a central aisle in which a steam powered traveller transported locomotives the full length of the Shop (Plate 3). Large sliding doors at each end of the centre aisle permitted the steam traveller to move outside to receive locomotives arriving at the south end of the Works for overhaul or repair. It was in this Shop that Patrick Stirling produced over 500 locomotives, including Doncaster's first locomotive completed in 1868, and his famous 8-foot 'Singles' from 1870.

Plate 3 - Erecting Shop Steam Traverser with Stirling 2-2-2 'Single'

Moving northwards across a large Wheel Yard and adjacent Iron Store stood the Smith Shop, a long L-shaped building containing 19 double and 15 single hearths. The Shop was also equipped with steam hammers and two furnaces, whilst outside was a boiler house for supplying steam for the hammers. The initial design of the Smithy appears to have underestimated the Works needs, as the Shop was soon extended during 1854 by the addition of a western flank to the building. Doncaster Works was certainly well equipped from its earliest days with facilities for forging and 'fire-welding' of wrought iron, but purchased all its iron castings from outside contractors until 1881. To the north of the Smithy separated by a narrow alleyway were the Wagon and Carriage Shops respectively. Built on a similar principle to the Erecting Shop, each with a central traveller feeding repair bays to either side. The Wagon Shop comprised

19 vehicle bays each side, with the traveller track extending across the alleyway between the east end of the Shop and the Turneries building, entering the latter through a large brick arch still visible today. The Carriage Shop adjoined the Wagon Shop on the north side and comprised a further 16 pairs of repair roads. To the west of the Wagon Shop were a timber store and two timber drying chambers.

The main workshops were separated from the offices and Turneries by an alleyway 26 feet wide running south to north. Railway lines were laid in the alleyway, with small turntables situated at points opposite the main entrance doors to the workshops. This permitted materials to be transported by railway wagon between the various workshops on the site. Whilst locomotives entered the Works from the south, carriages and wagons would be brought in from the North, a practice that largely remains to this day. Beyond the main workshops, smaller buildings contained a primitive fire engine and an early locomotive weigh house.

Much can be seen of the original 1853 works today. Denison House is largely in use as office accommodation, and the original Boiler Shop and Erecting Shops (further enlarged in 1866) form part of Wabtec Rail's wheel overhaul facilities. Doncaster Civic Trust successfully applied for both sets of buildings to be granted Grade II listing in 1986 in recognition of their historical importance (Plate 4). The original Smith Shop remains, with the exception of the western flank (demolished in 1965), and now forms part of Wabtec Rail's component overhaul division. The original Wagon and Carriage Shops were totally destroyed in an accidental fire in December 1940, and were rebuilt after the Second World War.

Works Enlargement - 1866

During Sturrock's time as Locomotive Engineer at Doncaster, the fleet of GNR locomotives grew to over 460. In order to keep pace with locomotive repairs in 1866 the original Erecting Shop was extended to the

Plate 4 - Early view of the Works

west by a further pair of six bays, making 42 in total. The original yard area between the Erecting Shop and Boiler Shop was roofed over to form a Tender Shop, equipped with hand-operated 35-ton cranes and machinery for slotting and drilling locomotive and tender frames. The Boiler Shop was extended by demolishing the internal walls of the Brass Foundry and Coppersmiths' Shop, and by construction of a new bay to the south, giving a doubling in Boiler Shop capacity. The enlarged Shop included the installation of a 'modern' riveting machine for boiler assembly. A new larger Brass Foundry with 12 crucible hearths was constructed to the west of the Boiler Shop near the Works boundary.

Further new workshops included a Spring Shop adjacent to the west end of the Smithy, comprising two furnaces and 12 hearths, making the Works self-sufficient in spring manufacture. Further to the west in the Crimpsall Yard a large Forge (Steam Hammer Shop) was constructed, housing three steam hammers and four furnaces. In an early example of energy conservation, the waste heat from the furnaces was used to power the boilers supplying steam to the hammers. At the rear of the Works site by the river, a new Gas Plant was constructed at a cost of £5,850, with 35 retorts, two 60 by 20 foot gasholders and capacity to supply gas for 6,000 lights. The original Carriage Shop in the north end of the Turneries was relocated to extended premises to the north, and the Main Carriage Shop was further extended in 1866 and 1873.

Archibald Sturrock was succeeded by Patrick Stirling as Locomotive Engineer in 1866. With the benefit of the enlarged locomotive facilities and in a change of GNR policy, Stirling was able to persuade the GNR Board to commence the construction of locomotives at Doncaster Works.

New Locomotive Shops - 1881 to 1891

A report commissioned by the company and undertaken by engineer John Ramsbottom in the late 1870's highlighted insufficient locomotive accommodation at Doncaster. A further major phase of workshop construction followed that was to relocate the focus of new locomotive manufacture from the original Erecting Shop to a new group of buildings around the area of the Forge in the Crimpsall Yard. In 1881 the Gas Works was further extended and an Iron Foundry was constructed near the then western boundary wall. A New Boiler Shop followed in 1882 situated between the Forge and Iron Foundry and a new Main Stores building was completed to the southwest of the Brass Foundry. The original Boiler Shop and Tender Shop were reorganised making a much-enlarged Tender construction and overhaul facility.

Despite the improved locomotive facilities, the old Erecting Shop of 1853 with its narrow aisles and short locomotive berths was becoming a major constraint as locomotives continued to grow in size. Therefore in 1891 a New Erecting Shop was completed

to the north west of the Forge. Each erecting bay could accommodate up to five locomotives on each of two outer roads, with a central outgoing road for finished locomotives, giving the shop a total capacity of 20 engines. The old Erecting Shop continued to carry out repairs and overhauls to the older and smaller Sturrock and Stirling engines.

Plate 5 - Works Yard Travelling Crane

The expansion of the locomotive facilities required the installation of additional machinery and a new Machine Shop was built in 1891 in the former Wheel Yard area between the original Erecting Shop and Smith Shop. This Shop was equipped with an impressive wheel lathe supplied by Smith, Beacock and Tannett for the turning of locomotive driving wheels (Plate 6).

Plate 6 - Smith, Beacock & Tannett Wheel Lathe

Carriage & Wagon Works Expansion - 1889 to 1891

By the early 1890's the Carriage Shops had become too small to cope with the increase in size of passenger coaches. Also the area around Doncaster station was becoming heavily congested with wagons awaiting Works repair. The first major change to relieve the wagon situation was the relocation in 1889 of wagon building and repair work to premises 1³/₄ miles to the south of The Plant at the Carr. The Carr Wagons Works comprised two main workshops and were the first shops at Doncaster to be illuminated by electric light. Workmen were taken to the Works by special train from Doncaster. To separate repair work from new construction, in 1890 the West Carriage Shop was built fronting the River Don, consisting of four low-roofed bays, each of three roads. Carriage lifting could be undertaken in a number of these bays, enabling repairs to be made to underframes, bogies and wheels. At the end of the Shop was a machining area comprising wheel and tyre lathes, wheel borers, axle lathes and wheel balancing equipment. Around this time a second workshop for light repairs and varnishing, the North Carriage Shed was completed at the northern end of the Works site.

extensive area of land on the Crimpsall meadows to the west of the Works, building work commenced in 1899. The new facilities comprised a Locomotive Paint Shop (south of the Iron Foundry), and a New Tender Shop and Locomotive Repair Shop situated well to the west of the site. Contractors H Arnold & Son, who again employed to construct the new locomotive repair facilities at a cost of £295,000. The 'Crimpsall' Repair Shop represented the latest thinking in locomotive shop design. Comprising four large bays 520 feet long for the dismantling and re-erection of locomotives, and two smaller machine bays, the Crimpsall Repair Shop could accommodate up to 100 locomotives.

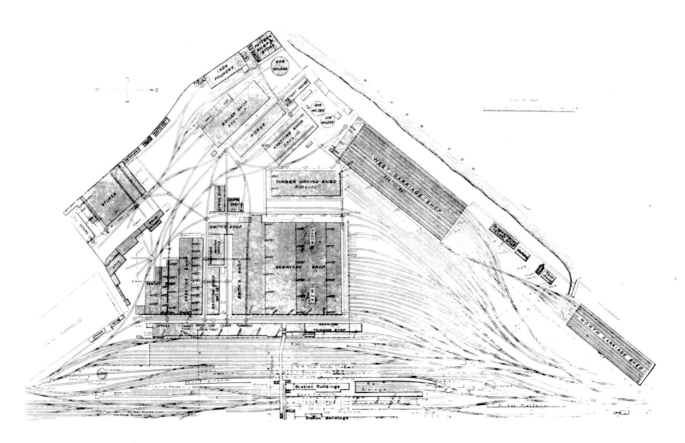

Plate7 - 1892 Plan of the Works

Further Locomotive Facilities - 1899 to 1902

Henry Ivatt had been appointed Locomotive Engineer of the Great Northern in 1896, following the death of Patrick Stirling. Although locomotives were required to return to Works for general overhaul or major repairs, a certain degree of independent thinking had developed at running depots. A custom and practice had arisen whereby The Plant would supply them with major components to undertake some Works-type repairs. Ivatt was dismayed at the primitive conditions in which this work was being performed and was able to persuade the GNR Board to authorise a further major expansion of locomotive facilities.

After protracted negotiations over the purchase of an

Beyond the traverser to the west was situated the New Tender Shop completed in 1900, comprising two large repair bays and a smaller machine bay. Two 20-ton overhead electric cranes were provided in each repair bay, with tenders being dismantled on a centre road in each bay. The Shop had a capacity to deal with up to 32 tenders on repair. The Locomotive Paint Shop completed in 1902, consisted of 8 roads with shallow pits, each road capable of holding up to 5 locomotives. The roof was of 'North Light' construction, designed to make the best use of the available natural light.

With the completion of the Crimpsall Repair Shops, the original Erecting Shop that since 1853 had been employed on the construction and repair of locomotives was therefore no longer needed. It would however continue in the construction of locomotive frames and new tenders, and later in the fabrication of new bogie and steel underframes for carriages.

Further Works Improvements

During the 1890's and early part of the 20th century, advances in technology enabled further improvements to be made to the buildings, plant and machinery within the Works. In 1895, the original Carmichael steam engines in the Turneries were replaced by modern compound condensing engines manufactured by Robey. 1896 saw the first widescale use of compressed air in the Boiler and Tender Shops where small shaft-driven compressors provided air for pneumatic caulking and chipping hammers and portable drills. The first Electric Power House was installed in the Lower Turnery between 1899 and 1900, comprising two 88 kW dynamos each coupled to two compound condensing steam engines. The demand for electric power increased substantially following the building of the Crimpsall Repair Shop with its all-electric cranes and traverser. Furthermore in 1901 the roof over the south bays of the West Carriage Shop was raised to allow the installation of two 20-ton electric cranes.

An additional steam engine and dynamo of 220 kW was installed in 1901, and again in 1903 and 1906 bringing capacity up to 836 kilowatts. Three Lancashire boilers supplied steam to these engines and to the 1895 Robey engine powering the machinery in the Upper Turnery. Increasing demand for hydraulic power within the Works led to the construction of a new central Hydraulic Power Station in part of the Forge building in 1902. The original accumulator from the New Boiler Shop was relocated and joined by a second unit, having a working pressure of 1500 psi supplied from two motor driven pumps. A 45-ton Ransome and Rapier 60 foot electric traverser was installed at the north end of the Main Carriage Shop in 1906 to enable the transfer of newly finished carriage bodies to the adjacent Carriage Paint Shop.

In early 1907 new drop hammers of 16 and 25 cwt capacity were installed in the Forge, fitted with Brett's patent steam lifter, and the practice of drop stamping certain steel components was introduced. In the same year, extensive alterations were undertaken in the New Boiler Shop to accommodate a new hydraulic riveter, manufactured by the Gloucester company of Messrs Fielding & Platt. The south end gable wall of the building was dismantled and the Shop extended, the new portion having a much higher roof line. By 1910 electrical demand at the Works was beginning to outstrip the available supply. New generating capacity became a necessity, and between 1910 and 1911 two diesel-powered generating plants were installed. The first was a 300 kW installation, in the northwest corner of the old Erecting Shop where part of the bay was partitioned off to form an Engine House. The second of 240 kW was on the north side of the Crimpsall Repair Shop.

The Plant at War - 1914 to 1918

Equipped with extensive numbers of machine tools, railway workshops were ideally suited to the manufacture of armaments and munitions during times of war. In 1915 part of the original Boiler Shop was reorganised for the reconditioning of 18 lb cartridge cases. Later in 1916, an area of the Lower Turnery was commandeered into use for the manufacture of 6 inch high explosive shell cases which were then taken for varnishing in the west end of the original Tender Shop. Much of this work was initially done by Apprentices, but as the war progressed more and more women were employed on shell production, often working 12-hour shifts including weekends. Women were also employed on more traditional railway work including carriage cleaning. Other work undertaken during the Great War included the construction of 750 ambulance stretchers in 1914 and a number of horse-drawn general purpose road wagons for the Army in 1915 in the Main Carriage Shop. Locomotive Engineer Nigel Gresley was subsequently awarded the CBE for his role in organising the Works for munitions production.

Last Years of the GNR - 1918 to 1923

Shortly after the end of the First World War, an agreement was made with Doncaster Corporation for the bulk supply of electricity to The Plant. As a result the two diesel engines and electric generators were sold. This arrangement would last until 1925 when the newly formed London & North Eastern Railway (LNER) negotiated with the Doncaster Collieries for a new high voltage supply. Feeder cables were laid from Potteric Carr in the south to a new Works Electric Power Station, where the supply voltage was stepped down and converted to 220 volts direct current. Overhead bare copper conductors then transmitted the supply to various parts of the Works. A similar arrangement was deployed at the Doncaster Carr Wagon Works.

By 1920, the lifting cranes in the New Erecting Shop and Crimpsall Repair Shops were nearing their safe working limits as locomotives grew in size and weight. The advent of new 6-foot diameter boilers on the Gresley-designed Class K3 2-6-0 locomotives resulted in the Erecting Shop cranes being converted from steam-driven rope to electric motor drive in 1921. The lifting chains were replaced by wire ropes and the main girders were strengthened to increase the working capacity from 30 to 45 tons. A similar strengthening modification was carried out on the two cranes in No 4 bay of the Crimpsall Repair Shop.

b) 1923 - 1948 London & North Eastern Railway

There was limited construction of new facilities at The Plant between the wars, with the exception of an extension to the Iron Foundry and a new Flanging

House equipped with oil-fired furnaces. However a major internal reorganisation of parts of the original 1853 Works was completed in 1932. This converted the original Erecting and Tender Shops into the Works Main Machine Shop, but retaining the top northwest aisle for locomotive frame manufacture. Over a period of time the machinery from the Upper and Lower Turneries was relocated to this Shop, including those for brass machining and finishing which were installed in the western end of the original steam traveller bay. Considerable savings were achieved in internal transportation costs by the new arrangements as before all materials had to be delivered to and from the Upper Turnery by hoist.

The locomotive repair facilities were also reorganised, including the adoption of the New Tender Shop for the heavy repair of boilers including superheater tubes. Tender overhaul and repair was relocated to two pits within No 1 bay of the Crimpsall Repair Shop, with the remainder of the bay becoming an axlebox manufacture and reconditioning area. Later, two bays of the Crimpsall were allocated solely for locomotive overhaul, with the third being used for heavy boiler repairs. The New Tender Shop boiler bay was then converted into an engine stripping area where locomotives would be partially dismantled before entering the Repair Shops.

In 1935, a new engine Weigh House was constructed between the Crimpsall and Paint Shop equipped with Voiron's patent weighing machines supplied by Ransome and Rapier. This replacing the original 1893 Denison weighing machines in the old Weigh House situated close to the station. About this time the Upper Turnery was converted into a Central Drawing Office, with separate offices for the Locomotive and Carriage & Wagon departments. A new central Compressor Station was commissioned in 1936 to cope with the increasing demand for compressed air. This was situated in the Locomotive Paint Shop, comprising three separate compressors directly coupled to 157 horsepower electric motors.

The Second World War and its Aftermath - 1939 to 1948

The outbreak of the Second World War put paid to any further development at the Works. However, in the late afternoon of Saturday 21st December 1940, an accidental fire broke out in the Main Carriage Shop. By early evening the whole of the Shop was well and truly ablaze from end to end. Fortunately the Carriage Paint Shop to the northeast corner of the Main Shop was saved. The area was eventually levelled to the ground and remained so until after the War. As in the First World War, the Works was heavily engaged on war work. With a seriously depleted male workforce, much female labour was again on both armaments and railway work. Work undertaken for the war effort included 4 inch high angle naval guns, tank gun mountings, anti-tank gun carriages, gun baseplates, 25

and 6 pounder breech rings, 'Crompton' anti-aircraft searchlights and 'Valentine' tank hulls. Compared to railway work, much tighter machining tolerances were needed for armaments work, and a number of machine tools were modified to give improved accuracy.

In 1947 construction commenced on a new Carriage Building Shop to replace the burnt down Main Carriage Shop. The new building comprised a steel frame structure with a central 'high bay' equipped with tandem overhead gantry cranes of 25-ton capacity, enabling carriages to be lifted over each other. Within the Carriage Building Shop complex were located a Sawmill, Joiners Shop, Trimming and Upholstery Shop and Fabrication and Assembly Areas. The economic hardships of War had left a legacy of under investment on the LNER and other railway companies, including a massive backlog of overhaul and repairs on locomotives and rolling stock. In 1948 the Government took control of the nation's railways, including its main workshops, and British Railways was born.

c) 1948 - 1968 British Railways

Under nationalisation, British Railways developed corporate locomotive policy that would have a significant effect on all its major workshops. Existing Doncaster produced locomotive designs would be replaced by a series of standard BR types with different Works being responsible for certain aspects of design, with manufacturing being shared across workshops. During this time there was considerable reorganisation of facilities at Doncaster to meet British Railways' requirements with a minimal amount of new buildings being constructed. One exception to this was during 1952 and 1953 when two steam raising plants were constructed, one near the Crimpsall Repair Shop for shop heating and the other situated near the west wall of the Carriage Paint Shop. In the early 1960s with the demise of steam traction, several areas of The Plant were re-organised to handle diesel-mechanical, diesel-electric and electric locomotives. Special low-level locomotive pits were constructed in the Crimpsall Repair Shop, to provide sufficient headroom to remove locomotive power units by overhead crane.

The West Carriage Shop and North Carriage Shed were converted for Diesel Multiple Unit (DMU) repairs and Electric Multiple Unit (EMU) construction. A Glass Fibre Shop, which produced items such as models of locomotive cabs, was established in part of the Pattern Shop (at the rear of the Iron Foundry). In addition, the Iron Foundry housed a Fettling Shop with a dust extraction plant to meet the Iron Foundry Regulations' requirements and a shot-blast cabinet for treating various components. With the end of steam locomotive work in 1963, several shops were converted to other uses. The Iron Foundry became a Crane and Chain Repair Shop, undertaking the overhaul of various types of cranes as well as the repair and testing of chains and lifting tackle, with the Boiler Shop becoming a Fabrication Shop. The Forge and original Spring Shop having outlived their usefulness were demolished along with the western end of the Smithy and a number of adjacent timber sheds. Spring work continued in the Brass Foundry and the Tender Shop, which over the previous 30 years had largely been concerned with boiler and stripping work, became a Locomotive Dismantling Shop.

During 1965 a Locomotive Test House was constructed to the east of the Crimpsall Shop to carry out fully graduated load tests on locomotives after building or repair. With full soundproofing, two locomotives of up to 4,000 hp could be tested simultaneously. The implementation of the British Railways Workshop Plan resulted in the termination of carriage building and classified repairs in the Main Carriage Shop in 1965. The Shop was reorganised into a Wagon Heavy Repair Shop, with the adjacent Carriage Paint Shop becoming a Wagon Light Repair Shop, with wagon work being transferred from the Carr Works back to The Plant after a gap of over 75 years .

Other new buildings erected during the 1960s to help cope with the workload instigated by the change over from steam to diesel included a Diesel Store adjacent to the Crimpsall Repair Shop, an Asbestos Shop for decontamination work and a DMU Test House between the North and West Carriage Shops. During this period these two repair shops became increasingly involved in DMU repair work. In the former 1891 Machine Shop close to the Main Offices, an Apprentice Training School was established. The Shop was equipped for the instruction of 80 craft trainees and comprised a training workshop and two classrooms, opening for the August 1964 apprentice intake. The apprentices spent one year in the School before continuing their training in the main workshops.

d) 1968 - 1987 British Rail Engineering Limited

Under the 1968 Transport Act, British Rail Engineering Limited (BREL) was formed as a wholly owned subsidiary company of the British Railways Board with Doncaster Works becoming one of 13 Works belonging to BREL. The Company's principal role was to overhaul and repair all locomotives, carriages and wagons in the BR fleet and to manufacture new locomotives and rolling stock. Furthermore all these facilities were to be made available to the private sector and overseas customers. Various Doncaster workshops became involved with private sector work, including the Main Machine Shop, Fabrication Shop and New Erecting Shop. During the 1970s there was also an updating of equipment in a number of workshops including investment in computer controlled machinery. A new air-conditioned Electronics Centre was built for the repair and calibration of a wide range of electronic components.

Later, the closure of BREL Works at Shildon, Horwich and Temple Mills led to an increase in wagon work coming to Doncaster and a substantial amount of money was spent on making the wagon facilities more efficient. Two new traversers were installed in the Wagon Shops in order to handle the increase in this kind of work. One traverser was an 'air cushion' type, which operated on much the same principal as a hovercraft, and was the first of its type in BR. This was situated at the south end of the Wagon Heavy Repair Shop. A second conventional traverser was installed externally across the north end of the wagon shops. The south end of the Wagon Heavy Repair Shop was organised as a central wheel shop for the whole site. This included facilities for dynamic balancing of wheels and ultrasonic flaw detection in axles. Other

Plate 8 – Plan of the Works 1962

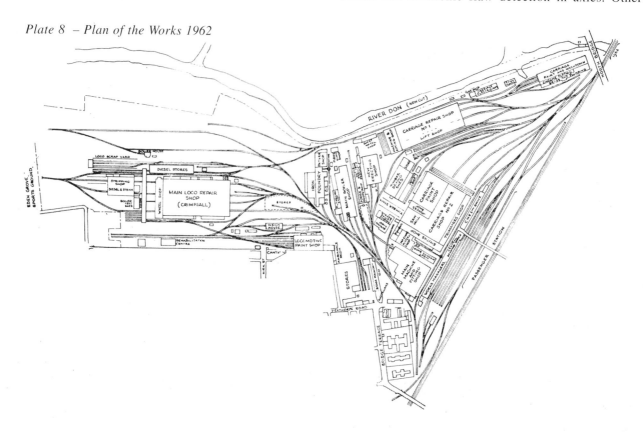

new equipment included three new gantry cranes, an extra skimming lathe for turning disc brakes of 'Merry-Go-Round' coal wagon wheels, another wheel profiling lathe and improved bearing cleaning equipment.

With the commencement of Class 58 locomotive construction in the early 1980s, a specially designed Asquith 'travelling' gantry drilling and milling machine was installed in the New Erecting Shop for the machining of the locomotive underframe. To improve working practices in the DMU Shops a Tempest & Dibbs Tunnel Wash Machine was fitted. This enabled bogies to be cleaned without the need for stripping and was also used for the cleaning of DMU and wagon components during repair and overhaul.

e) 1986 - 1987 Major Re-organisation & Emergence of the NSC, BRML and RFS Industries

A new locomotive and rolling stock 'Manufacturing and Maintenance' policy was introduced by the British Railways Board in the early 1980's. This was to have major consequences for Doncaster Works and its subsequent role. Competitive procurement was proposed for vehicle manufacture and all Heavy General Repairs, and a new policy of component exchange at Depots was adopted. A National Supply Centre (NSC) was to be established to furnish all depots with spares. Under the existing regime eight BREL Works supplied BR with components but this system had proved far from satisfactory. To implement the new policy BREL was split into two, with eight of the original 13 Works to remain. Of these, four sites were to become part of British Rail Maintenance Limited (BRML) with the remaining four dealing with new construction and heavy overhaul work. In 1986 following the announcement of these proposals Doncaster Works faced closure for the first time in over 130 years.

Establishment of the National Supply Centre (NSC)

Faced with the threat of imminent closure, several BREL personnel worked earnestly to retain some form of railway activity at the Works. With a view to proposing a site to BR for the new NSC, Doncaster's DMU repair areas were vacated and the work accommodated elsewhere in the Works. Amongst the alternative sites submitted to BR for the NSC, Doncaster was chosen because it had many advantages over its rivals. The DMU Repair Shop (former West Carriage Shop) was designated as the Main Warehouse for the NSC, and extensive work was undertaken during late 1986 to convert and refurbish the former workshop to its new role. The Works site was segregated and fenced and a separate access road was constructed during 1987 into the NSC. This entered the site from Hexthorpe Road between the Brass Foundry and Stores building to the west of the existing Works' entrance, requiring the clearance of a number of ancillary buildings. The Central Power House (which had been built on the site of the 1866 Forge, demolished 1965) was pulled down in July 1987 to permit extension of the road to the new loading bay at the west end of the Main Warehouse (behind the New Erecting Shop and on the site of the original 1866 Gas Works).

The NSC was opened in late 1987 to provide a spares and parts service to over 100 BR Depots, including a 24-hour service for urgent items called Urgent Vehicle Standing (UVS) orders. Over 1,000,000 different items were held in stock with a value of around £100 million. 230 Works staff were employed at the NSC to handle over 1,200 orders every day. Delivery of items was to be mainly by road but rail access to the warehouses was retained. Large items such as power units, bogies and wheelsets were not held on site but controlled by the NSC and moved directly between manufacturers and repairers and the Depots. The NSC's 'nerve centre' was initially based in the old Canteen buildings in Kirk Street, and was equipped with the latest computer technology to manage the extensive range of stock.

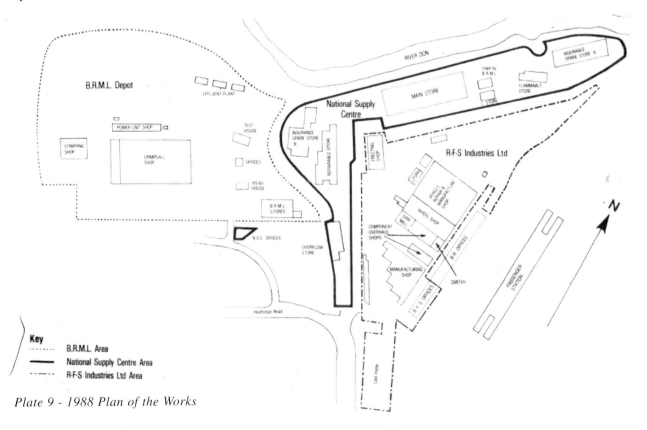

Key
.... B.R.M.L. Area
———— National Supply Centre Area
—··—··— R·F·S Industries Ltd Area

Plate 9 - 1988 Plan of the Works

New BRML Level 5 Depot

The BREL management members in Doncaster were also looking to retain some locomotive and rolling stock overhaul activity wherever practicable. Consequently, certain areas involved in heavy overhaul and repairs were reorganised under the newly formed British Rail Maintenance Limited (BRML) as a 'Level 5' Maintenance Depot. Under Level 5 status, Doncaster would continue undertaking classified repair of rolling stock and the heavy overhaul of locomotives. The areas within the BRML facility included the Crimpsall Repair Shop, Dismantling Shop (former Tender Shop), Diesel Stores, Test House, Weigh House, Locomotive Paint Shop and Electronics Centre.

Emergence of RFS Industries Limited (RFS)

During the autumn of 1986 an exciting scheme began to take shape led by four members of the BREL Doncaster management team, Steve Hinton, Paul Page, Barry Pierce and David Theyers. They had been involved with the establishment of the NSC and BRML Depot and foresaw that once these were established, there was going to be an area of Doncaster Works which might not be retained by BREL or accommodated within BRML. This area included many of the original 19th century Great Northern buildings and the work within them, which at this time was mainly concerned with wheel overhaul, wagon building and repair. This type of work was being relinquished by British Railways, and as the political climate was right, an opportunity existed for a 'management buy-out' of the remaining business. The four managers formed a new company called RFS Industries Limited and set about obtaining the necessary financial backing. Separately, and as a prelude to sale, the BR Board had removed the site from under BREL's control and established it on 24th May 1987 as Doncaster Wagon Works Limited. The business was put up for sale, and was eventually purchased by RFS Industries on 16th October 1987.

An entire area of the Works which had been threatened with complete closure now appeared to have a healthier future. The buildings taken over by RFS included the Wagon Heavy and Light Repair Shops (former 1949 Main Carriage Shop and old Carriage Paint Shop), New Erecting Shop (1891), Main Machine Shop (original 1853 Erecting Shop) and Maintenance Shop (originally the 1891 Machine Shop and later Apprentice Training School), Smiths Shop (1853), Damper Shop (part of the Smiths Shop), former Brass Foundry (1866), Saw Mill and Wheel Overhaul facility (within the Heavy Repair Shop). The Works buildings (Denison House) fronting on to the main line were retained by BR as office accommodation under the management of the BR Property Board. RFS Industries rented the southern part of Denison House (including the 1853 Locomotive Engineer's offices) to accommodate its management, engineering and support staff.

f) 1987 - 1993 RFS Industries

Shortly after its purchase of the remaining workshop areas of The Plant, RFS Industries developed into a wider based group. RFS Engineering Limited was formed comprising four divisions, namely Vehicles, Manufacturing, Wheelsets and Components representing the well-established overhaul and repair services to be found in a main Works.

Over time the name RFS became recognised in the industry and the company enjoyed early success with a number of rail vehicle projects. During this time a new vehicle paint facility was erected in the middle of the site, in the area of the former timber sheds between the Light Shop and New Erecting Shop. In 1988 a 'wet blast' cleaning building was constructed to the north of the Heavy Shop for the pre-cleaning of rail vehicles. In 1989 RFS

Engineering bought the business of industrial locomotive builders Thomas Hill of Kilnhurst near Rotherham. This included the manufacture and repair of shunting locomotives, including the historic name of Sentinel. Shunter work was initially transferred from Doncaster Works to the Thomas Hill site, but a shrinking market led to the work being brought back to Doncaster and the eventual closure of the Kilnhurst facility in 1993.

RFS had looked to diversify from a sole dependency upon BR for its workload, and had entered into a major refurbishment contract with London Underground Limited (LUL) for the complete refurbishment of its 'C' (Metropolitan & Circle Line) stock trains in 1989. This contract, extending over 4 years and valued at over £25 million, provided for an extensive refurbishment, including new bogies and a complete interior remodelling. The work was undertaken throughout the RFS Works, including the New Erecting Shop (bodywork) and Light Shop (interior work).

In the early 1990's RFS suffered a number of setbacks in its ambitions. With the prospect of railway privatisation on the horizon, there was a general reduction in BR's requirement for vehicle overhaul, including 'Merry-Go-Round' wagon work. Difficulties were also being experienced on the original LUL contract and a subsequent order for '1973 Stock' (Piccadilly Line) refurbishment with a combined value of over £100 million. Coming at a time of general manufacturing recession, this resulted in the company running into financial difficulties due to under capitalisation. Despite everyone electing to take a 5% pay cut to try and reduce the company's costs, RFS went into receivership in December 1993, a particularly bitter blow for all those who had tried to keep the company afloat.

g) 1987 - 2003 National Supply Centre, Formation of Railpart (UK) Limited, Purchase by Unipart

The initial warehousing at the National Supply Centre was centred in the DMU Repair Shop (former West Carriage Shop) but from the early days of operation it was clear that the volume of parts to be stored and handled by the NSC would exceed the available space within these premises. Within 6 months of opening, the redundant North Carriage Shed building was re-commissioned into service and by the end of 1988 this too was full. The volume of slow moving and safety stock spares that was eventually consigned to the NSC overwhelmed the original warehousing capacity. Over the next 5 years further storage space was rented on a temporary basis at the BRML workshops at Springburn (Glasgow) and Eastleigh (Southampton) to help alleviate the problem.

By 1988, the establishment of the NSC was delivering significantly reduced lead times in the 'repair loop' by up to 5 weeks. Additional benefits were also derived from the economy of scale in holding one 'pool' of float material versus the many that had previously existed. The BR practice of repairing all components as soon as they came off vehicles had therefore become largely inappropriate and the business adopted a demand-driven philosophy repairing only those spares it could trade-in within the lead-time of the overhaul.

To accommodate this change the NSC acquired further buildings on The Plant site. This included the Fabrication Shop (former Boiler Shop of 1882) which became the Repair Store into which unrepaired components would be held until customer demand required them to be shipped to a repairer. Adjacent to the Repair Store in the Chain Shop & Baler Store were placed slow moving or insurance spares stores. Other buildings within today's Railpart complex that lie between the Main Warehouse (the former DMU Shop/original West Carriage Shop) and the former North Carriage Shed are the Asbestos Shop which is now a workshop consumables store and the Test House which is largely a quarantine store. In January 1990 the NSC's main offices were relocated from Kirk Street into refurbished accommodation in the former 1853 Turneries building fronting Doncaster station, which was named 'Denison House'. Around 1993 a new Glass Store was constructed adjacent to the riverbank.

The NSC were initially loaned the suite of buildings of the original 1882 Stores to the west of the new access road into the site. Comprising the Damper Shop, Nos 5 & 8 Stores and the former DM & EE Training Centre, these buildings were eventually transferred to NSC ownership. The need for slow moving and insurance spare storage was not diminishing and the eventual relocation of inventory from Glasgow and Eastleigh Works was to create a long-term need for this area of warehousing. In 2003, Nos 5 & 8 Stores provide warehousing for new Siemens' business whilst the Training Centre is an archive store.

From its inception and through the early 1990's the National Supply Centre continued to consolidate spare parts from BR's main workshops and commenced supply to around 90 train maintenance depots across the UK. The NSC operated as an internal commercial business within BR and sold parts to its customers. As the pace of commercialisation of the rail industry gathered momentum in the lead up to privatisation, the National Supply Centre took the name Railpart (UK) Ltd, becoming a wholly owned subsidiary of the British Railways Board in March 1995. During the privatisation process the 6 BRML workshops were sold with contracts in place to overhaul spare parts for Railpart. These contracts were subsequently put out to tender as a competitive market place developed.

Railpart (UK) Limited was sold to the Unipart Group of Companies in 1997, who brought key skills, tools and techniques in demand chain management from the automotive sector, where it had itself been privatised from the public sector. During 1998 a number of existing contracts that had been in place since privatisation came to an end. These were all successfully renegotiated and a number of new contracts were won. Railpart has since continued to develop its business, including a large investment in SAP business systems and a re-engineering of its business processes. This has led to a significant improvement in the availability of 'off-the-shelf' spares for its customers. Unipart's philosophy of continuous improvement has led to the development of the Railpart Technical Dossier as a principal method of specification control with its suppliers. Most recently, Railpart has entered the new trains arena with a long-term contract with Siemens to support new 'Desiro' trains for South West Trains and First Great Eastern and has been successful in securing orders from a wide range of non-UK customers.

h) 1987 - 2003 BRML Doncaster Level 5 Depot, Purchase by ABB/Adtranz now Bombardier Transportation

Under BRML, Doncaster Level 5 Depot became a centre for the cost-effective heavy maintenance of vehicles for British Rail. Comprising 45 acres of the Works site, the Depot was reorganised with activities being principally centred on the Crimpsall Repair Shop. Bays 1, 1A and 2 were reorganised for the repair and overhaul of DMU's and Non-Passenger Coaching Stock with Bays 3, 3A and 4 being used for locomotive work. At one end of No 3 Bay locomotive bogie repairs were undertaken with the other end used for heavy

fabrication and welding work. Refurbishment of locomotive traction motors took place in Bay 3A with No 4 Bay reserved for the cost-effective maintenance repairs and examinations of shunting and main line diesel-electric locomotives. During this period, BRML Doncaster Depot Managers included Frank Frith, Ron Price and Phil Crawshaw.

The painting of locomotives was relocated from the Paint Shop to the Crimpsall Shop and in time to the DMU Power Unit Repair Shop. The Paint Shop then became a store for a period before being eventually mothballed. With the closure of ABB's York Carriage Works in 1995, office accommodation was installed in Bays 1A and 3A in the Crimpsall Repair Shop. This was to enable EMU work to be transferred from York, with some staff travelling from their home base until the contract was completed. With the commencement of BR privatisation in 1994, the six BRML Depots were identified as early candidates for sale. In June 1995, the BRML Doncaster facility was privatised, being purchased by ABB (Asea Brown Boveri Ltd) of Zurich, Switzerland. This was in addition to other workshop facilities purchased at Ilford and Chart Leacon (Ashford, Kent), which were formed into ABB Customer Support Limited.

The new ownership brought a change of emphasis in the Depot's activities in what had became a very competitive market. A major reorganisation of staff was undertaken, including reduction in the size of the workforce from 750 to 350. During this period a number of changes were made within the facility, including improvements to the site and the removal of redundant equipment. This included the sale of the Accounts and Stores offices housed in portable buildings near the Kirk Street entrance and the demolition of E1 offices and the Rehabilitation Centre. The Goliath Crane in between the Crimpsall Shops and the River Don was dismantled and two 45-ton cranes in the Stripping/Dismantling Shop (former New Tender Shop) were sold to a private company. In this period the Stripping Shop became known as the Ancillary Workshop and for a period was used for the heavy cleaning of Class 91 underframes.

On 1 January 1996 the railway activities of ABB were merged with Daimler-Benz of Stuttgart in Germany, to form Adtranz (ABB Daimler-Benz Transportation). The new venture had a worldwide workforce of around 22,000 employees, and marketing, design and production facilities in 40 countries. The group's product portfolio ranged from electric and diesel locomotives, ICE and X2000 high-speed Intercity to regional trains, trams and underground vehicles, people movers, signal and traffic control systems, fixed installations in addition to servicing and maintenance.

Under a major reorganisation of the Adtranz Doncaster site in early 1996, there was a grouping together of all activities of each main product group. This included the re-location of heavy machines within the former locomotive area of Bay 4 in the Crimpsall Repair Shop, to help speed the throughput of modifications and collision repairs. The Test House remained regularly in use for both locomotives and multiple units, and there were a number of stored locos on the site as a source of spares for rebuild programmes.

The Weigh House was dismantled in October 1997 the year in which the Voiron equipment was donated to the National Railway Museum in York. Weighing of locos was moved to inside the Crimpsall Repair Shop at the east end of No 4 bay using rail-mounted electronic load cells. In 2001 a 25kV overhead catenary was installed outside the Crimpsall for the testing of GNER Class 91 electric locomotives following heavy overhaul and repair, to avoid unnecessary shunting of locomotives to and from the West Yard opposite the station for testing.

In 2000, Adtranz, together with Alstom, signed a contract with HSBC Rail for the major refurbishment of 31 Class 91 locomotives on lease to Great North Eastern Railway (GNER). Classified as Heavy General Repairs, the work entailed a substantial overhaul of the locomotive and its systems including a number of reliability-centred modifications and improvements. The work was carried out at Doncaster, starting in July 2000 and was completed in April 2003.

On May 1st 2001, Bombardier Transportation acquired Adtranz, creating the global leader in the rail equipment manufacturing and servicing industry. Bombardier Transportation's wide range of products includes passenger rail vehicles and total transit systems. It also manufactures locomotives, freight cars, propulsion and controls and provides rail control solutions. Headquartered in Montreal, Canada with European headquarters in Berlin, Germany, Bombardier Transportation employs 36,000 people and has manufacturing facilities in 23 countries.

Bombardier Transportation is a unit of Bombardier Inc., a Canadian-based diversified manufacturing and services company, world-leading manufacturer of business jets, regional aircraft, and motorised recreational products. The Corporation also provides financial services and asset management in business areas aligned with its core expertise.

The Doncaster site of Bombardier Transportation specialises primarily in the repair and modernisation of rail vehicles. This has included passenger vehicle overhaul of DMU's owned by Angel Trains and operated by Northern Spirit, Central Trains, Wales & West and First North Western. The site is also responsible for the heavy maintenance support of

HSBC's Class 91 fleet in operation with GNER.

i) 1994 - 2003 Launch of RFS(E) Limited, Purchase by WABCO, Renaming as Wabtec Rail Limited

Price Waterhouse were appointed as receivers for the RFS group of companies, and there followed a prolonged period of trading under the Receiver during 1994. This culminated in the sale of the passenger side of the business, some 80% of the company's then current turnover of £50 million, in the summer of 1994 to Bombardier ProRail. The buyers took on the residual completion of the second LUL contract including the associated staff and assets, relocating the work to their site in Horbury, Wakefield. With the senior management no longer in place, the residual business and assets left at Doncaster were acquired by a team of former middle management who re-christened the company RFS(E) Limited. The new management team developed a strategy which concentrated on the core activities for which there was management and artisan expertise, well-equipped facilities and most importantly, a market. RFS(E) began life on 8th November 1994, headed by John Meehan (Commercial Director), Robert Johnson (Finance Director), Michael Bostock (Operations Director) and Martin Pridmore (Fleetcare Director). The team was further strengthened by the appointment of Michael Roe as Engineering Director in 1997.

A key ingredient in reviving the fortunes of RFS(E) was that during receivership, not one customer was lost. This customer loyalty offered the chance to perpetuate an ongoing cash income, rather than having to start the business from scratch. It was also a factor that convinced the four directors to continue with the well-known initials, albeit in a slightly modified form RFS(E), to enable the new company to be registered. The management buy-out saved 180 jobs and in the new company's first year it secured an order book worth over £10 million. One of the major assets removed from the Doncaster site by Bombardier was the vehicle paint facility. In order to ensure continuity of vehicle overhaul and associated painting work, a new state-of-the-art paint

Plate 10 –Valiant 0-6-0 Locomotive (fitted with remote control capability)

booth was purchased by RFS(E) in 1995 and installed within the shell of the building formerly used for 'wet-blast' cleaning of vehicles. An opportunity was also taken to dismantle various disused outbuildings, including the former Power House near the Light Repair Shop. Between 1996 and 1998, the major focus of wheelset overhaul was moved from the south end of the Heavy Shop into the former Main Machine Shop (the original Boiler and Erecting Shops of 1853). This was to provide a more suitable environment for the overhaul of wheelsets and to allow for future growth of the wheel business. During receivership, the company's main offices had been relocated from rented offices at the south end of Denison House, to various operational offices about the site. In 1996/7, the Heavy Shop stores (the Trimming Shop of the rebuilt 1949 Main Carriage Shop) were refurbished to form a company office suite.

Following the success of RFS(E), the management buy-out team looked for long term security for the company. Thus in the autumn of 1997, they sought a buyer for the company turning their attention to the United States. This resulted in the company being acquired by the Westinghouse Air Brake Company (WABCO) on 5 April 1998. WABCO traces its origins back to the invention of the straight air brake by George Westinghouse, with headquarters at the original 1870 Westinghouse factory site in Wilmerding on the outskirts of Pittsburgh, Pennsylvania.

Purchase by WABCO has brought new investment into the Doncaster site, including the re-roofing of the Heavy Shop and part of the Light Shop. New wheelset overhaul equipment includes a wheelset blast cleaning cabinet, axle bearing cleaning plant and a magnetic particle inspection rig for complete wheelsets. During 2001, the company's component overhaul business has been consolidated from the workshops at the rear of the former Apprentice Training School (1891 Machine Shop) into a fully refurbished facility housed in the 1853 Smiths Shop. This includes the equipping of an Electronics Service Centre for the overhaul of the Corporation's 'black box' data recorders. The former Apprentice Training School classrooms have been refurbished to provide a modern Training Centre facility.

In October 1999, following a merger between WABCO and another US railroad equipment supplier, the name Wabtec Corporation (Westinghouse Air Brake Technologies Corporation) was adopted. To reflect RFS(E)'s role within the Corporation it was appropriate to rename the company Wabtec Rail Limited on 1st March 2000, adopting the new corporate identification in place of the familiar blue RFS logo.

3 Locomotive Construction and Overhaul Great Northern Railway 1853-1923

Archibald Sturrock was appointed as Locomotive Engineer of the GNR in March 1850, and occupied the post when the Company moved its Boston Works to Doncaster in 1853. He had previously served as Works Manager under Daniel Gooch at the Great Western Railway (GWR) Works at Swindon, and a personal testimonial from Isambard Kingdom Brunel had helped him secure the position on the Great Northern. Sturrock was able to draw on his GWR experience when developing the new facilities at Doncaster. GNR policy of the time was to purchase locomotives from outside contractors, rather than build within their own workshops. Initially, locomotives were bought to manufacturers' proprietary designs, but Sturrock soon began to specify his own requirements. An order from R & W

Hawthorn of Newcastle for 12 large sandwich-framed 2-2-2's, for delivery in 1853-4, can really be called Sturrock's first passenger design for the GNR.

Sturrock was determined to design engines for the GNR that could match the speeds of the broad gauge GWR locomotives and enable the Great Northern to compete effectively with the rival London & North Western Railway. He favoured larger fireboxes and higher boiler pressures than was generally the norm at the time. He was sometimes hampered in his desire to have the most appropriate

Plate 11 - Archibald Sturrock

locomotive power by the Great Northern Board's reluctance to order well in advance of requirements.

In his determination to show what could be achieved, Sturrock obtained the Board's permission for Hawthorn to build a 2-2-2-2, which would get passengers from London to Edinburgh in eight hours. Number 215, delivered in August 1853, owed much to Gooch's GWR designs, but initially suffered from derailment problems due to its rigid wheelbase. This led to the hasty installation of a leading bogie, or what Sturrock called 'a moveable carriage in front', making the locomotive a 4-2-2 wheel arrangement. The locomotive was significantly ahead of its time and Patrick Stirling's later single-wheelers had many similar features.

On the GNR the flimsy iron rails had been a distinct impediment to locomotive design. In order to increase the pulling power of his 0-6-0 tender engines without adding to their axle weight, Sturrock experimented with turning the dead weight of the tender into an additional steam engine. This auxiliary engine being supplied with steam through a flexible pipe over 22 feet in length from the same boiler as the locomotive. Initial experiments indicated that locomotives with steam tenders could pull 60 wagons compared to the standard 40, suggesting that significant savings could be made. Unfortunately, these 'double' engines were unpopular with locomotive crews, who were constantly bathed in steam and heat on the footplate, and with their much-enlarged fireboxes and boilers proved to be expensive to maintain. Increasing failures led to a shortage of available locomotives and a loss of confidence in Sturrock's management of the locomotive department at Doncaster.

By the autumn of 1865 Sturrock intimated to the GNR Board of his intention to retire at the end of 1866 at the relatively young age of 50. Patrick Stirling had been recruited from the Glasgow & South Western Railway to the vacant Works Manager's position at Doncaster in early 1866, but on 1st October of that year the GNR Locomotive Committee decided that 'Mr Stirling should take charge of the Locomotive Department forthwith, Mr Sturrock to remain to the end of the year as Consulting Engineer'. Following Stirling's appointment as Locomotive Engineer, further orders for steam tenders were cancelled in favour of 'conventional' locomotives, and existing locomotives were gradually rebuilt and stripped of their steam tender equipment.

Stirling benefited from the newly enlarged locomotive facilities at the Plant and in April 1867 was successful in securing permission from the GN Board for the construction of three 0-4-2 mixed-traffic tender locomotives at Doncaster. Designated as Class F2, locomotive No 18 was completed on 3rd January 1868 almost a year from Stirling's appointment and the first of 709 engines to be built at the Plant to his designs. In addition to new locomotive manufacture, there was also a considerable amount of work undertaken rebuilding and standardising older Sturrock engines, together with a regular programme of general repairs.

Stirling did much to restore the confidence of the GN Board in the Locomotive Department at Doncaster. By the adoption of standard designs and components he was able to reduce the costs of new locomotive construction by a considerable margin. Stirling's locomotives were characterised by their straight-backed domeless boilers (with the regulator fitted in the smokebox), brass safety valve covers, brass rimmed splashers, narrow rounded cabs and handsome built-up chimneys.

One of the finest examples of Stirling's designs was his 4-2-2 express passenger engine of which the first, No 1 built in 1870, was Doncaster's fiftieth locomotive. These engines became known as 'Eight Footers' or 'Singles' because of their

eight-foot diameter driving wheels and they displayed many of Stirling's design characteristics. Many of these locomotives were built in twos at Doncaster, incorporating design improvements with each pair manufactured. A total of 53 4-2-2 and 2-2-2 'Singles' were built at Doncaster across most of Stirling's reign. Besides being celebrated for his high-speed passenger locomotives, Stirling was also noted for a 0-6-0 goods engine that he designed in 1871. This engine was reputed to be capable of hauling a loaded train of 55 wagons with a total weight of over 600 tons. Other Stirling designs included 2-4-0 secondary main-line engines and 0-4-2 and later 0-4-4 tank engines for London and West Riding suburban services.

Stirling died suddenly in 1895, at the age of 75 whilst still holding office. After an interregnum of four months, his successor, Henry Alfred Ivatt, took up the position as Locomotive Superintendent. Ivatt was trained at Crewe and formerly occupied the position of District Locomotive Superintendent of the Southern Division of the Great Southern & Western Railway at Cork. Ivatt's son-in-law OVS Bulleid was later to recall that on appointment Ivatt had walked the entire 156 miles of the GNR main line, and seeing the inferior quality of the track remarked that 'he wished he was back in Ireland'! It was this that prompted Ivatt to abandon the principal of single leading wheels in favour of leading bogies on his locomotives to provide extra stability.

Ivatt was immediately faced with the task of meeting the demand for more powerful engines, occasioned by the rapidly increasing goods traffic and heavier passenger trains. Ivatt designed 10 different types of locomotives during his 15-year term of office. These included 4-4-2, 0-8-2 and 0-6-2 suburban tank engines and for passenger duties both 4-4-0 coupled engines and 4-2-2 singles, a more powerful adaptation of Stirling's design. The last Single, delivered in 1901 was the last 4-2-2 produced for any British railway company.

In early 1897 Ivatt outlined his design for an elongated more powerful engine with the unprecedented 4-4-2 wheel

Plate 12 - On the 30th December 1903, and in the fiftieth year of The Plant, Archibald Sturrock (right) visited Henry Ivatt. The pair are photographed in front of Ivatt Class K1-0-8-0 'Long Tom' No 405

arrangement. American 4-4-2 engines had won fame for their high-speed performances between Camden and Atlantic City, and the wheel arrangement became synonymous with the name 'Atlantic'. Ivatt's first Atlantic of 1898 was No 990 'Henry Oakley', named after the recently retired GNR General Manager. The Canadian Yukon gold rush in the Klondike Valley of 1896 was big news of the time, and the class gained the nickname 'Klondikes'. Ivatt also designed a class of powerful 0-8-0 tank engines, delivered from 1900 onwards, utilising the boiler of the 'Klondikes', nicknamed 'Long Toms' after a long-barrelled naval gun of the period.

In 1902, Ivatt was to design an even larger Atlantic No 251 with a massive 5' 6" diameter boiler. He also experimented with early forms of superheating to gain greater locomotive efficiency and economy, and with different forms of compound (high and low pressure cylinders) locomotives, although the latter experiments were inconclusive. His Atlantic locomotives, later fitted with superheating which added greatly to their performance, were the mainstay of the Great Northern express passenger services for over 20 years until replaced by Gresley's Pacific locomotives from 1922 onwards.

The Great Northern experimented with the concept of steam Railmotors in 1905, comprising a small steam locomotive and passenger coach on a common articulated underframe. This enabled trains to work in either push or pulling mode on lightly used branch lines. Of six Railmotors purchased by the GNR, four were supplied by outside contractors and two manufactured at Doncaster by way of cost comparison. The carriages for the Doncaster-built Railmotors were the first designed by young Herbert Nigel Gresley, appointed as GNR Carriage and Wagon Superintendent in the same year. The Railmotor's steam engines were finally scrapped in 1927, but the carriages were converted into twin articulated coaches, the last pair remaining in service until 1958.

In September 1911, Ivatt retired at the age of 60 at the height of his powers, and was succeeded by Nigel Gresley (Plate 14), who had since 1905 made a name for himself in the Carriage and Wagon Department. He was trained at Crewe and had worked at Horwich, Blackpool and Newton Heath before arriving at Doncaster. Gresley, who took up his post in August with Ivatt staying on in an advisory role until the year end, set about strengthening his personnel team including the appointment of Oliver Bulleid (who had started as a premium apprentice at Doncaster in 1901) as his personal technical assistant.

Ivatt had left the Great Northern with a fine stable of fast powerful Atlantic passenger locomotives, and the pressing need for Gresley was to improve the GN's fleet of freight locomotives. His first design, emerging from the Plant in 1912 was a 2-cylinder 2-6-0 'Mogul', later designated Class

K1, and the first mainline Doncaster design to be fitted with Walschaerts valve gear. This was followed shortly afterwards in 1913/4 by the Class O1 2-8-0 mineral engine. Both these designs were both rugged and successful from the start but suffered from poor riding characteristics, becoming nicknamed 'Ragtimers' and 'Tangos' respectively after popular dances of the day.

During the First World War, Gresley carried out experiments with multi-cylinder engines in an attempt to produce more efficient and powerful locomotives. The result of this work appeared in 1918 when a three cylinder 2-8-0 mineral locomotive No 461, similar in design to the Class O1, was built at the Plant. Apart from the unusual choice of three cylinders, giving more evenly distributed forces and less track damage, the main design characteristic was the gear for actuating the inside cylinder valves. This was derived from the two sets of 'outside' Walschaerts gear by a series of rocking shafts. Although Gresley was criticised for the over-complicated design, two years later this feature was developed further by Gresley, assisted by H Holcroft, and applied to the three-cylinder Class K3. Similar in design to the Class K1, but in place of the rocking shafts a simplified conjugated gear in the form of rocking levers in the ratio 2:1 was used. The locomotive was also the first one in Britain to be fitted with a 6ft diameter boiler and is seen as a transition to his larger and more powerful Pacific-type passenger locomotives.

Gresley's next major stride in British locomotive construction came in March 1922 when his first 'Pacific' 4-6-2 engine, Class A1 No. 1470 was completed at the Works. Designed to haul 600-ton trains at an average speed of 50 mph, the locomotive was named 'Great Northern' even before it had left the Plant. It was followed in June 1922 by No 1471 named Sir Frederick Banbury after GNR Chairman and vociferous opponent of the impending grouping of the Great Northern into the London & North Eastern Railway. 10 further Pacifics were ordered, hastened by the impending grouping and completed before the end of 1923, including No 4472 'Flying Scotsman'. Their introduction proved to be the pinnacle of GNR locomotive design as on 1st July 1923, the Company amalgamated with the east coast group of railway companies to become the LNER.

LNER 1923-1948

The early successful performance of the Class A1's ensured that Gresley's design was the LNER's preferred choice of Pacific locomotive over the North Eastern Railway A2 Pacific designed by Sir Vincent Raven. Flying Scotsman was exhibited at the British Empire Exhibition at Wembley in 1924, alongside the Great Western Railway's Caerphilly Castle. The GW engine bore the plaque 'The most powerful

Plate 13 - Newly built Steam Railmotors Nos 1 & 2 (Doncaster built, right) and 7 & 8 (Avonside built, left) stand outside the Crimpsall in December 1905.

locomotive in the British Isles'. A debate raged between the two companies and led to a series of Interchange trials conducted on each other's main lines in May 1925. Unfortunately the LNER got off to a bad start with troubles due to overheated bearings and defective sanders. The GW locomotives generally outperformed the Gresley locomotives both in terms of economy and timings.

This was a salutary lesson for Gresley, who had been cautious in his design of the Class A1, using somewhat small 9" piston valves and a conservative boiler pressure of 180 psi. The valve travel and lap were also shorter due to problems experienced with valve over travel on the earlier Class K3.

After numerous trials, 'long lap' valves were authorised to be fitted to all existing Class A1s in 1927, as well as to those under construction. This modification and subsequent reduction of up to 20% in coal consumption was probably one of the factors that contributed to the introduction on 1st May 1928, of the non-stop 'Flying Scotsman service between King's Cross and Edinburgh. To complete this journey of 392 miles without stopping was one of the greatest feats of locomotive endurance ever achieved. Gresley designed a special locomotive tender fitted with a corridor and a vestibule connection, and is reported to have laid out his tables and chairs in his office to perfect the design which he patented in 1928. These features enabled a spare crew, travelling in the first compartment of a train to gain access to the locomotive and relieve the first crew, half way through the journey. Gresley also reappraised his thoughts on boiler design, and successful trials were made with two boilers designed for a pressure of 220 psi. As a result, 10 new Pacifics of 1928/9 were fitted with the higher-pressure boiler and larger 20" cylinders, being classified as A3 instead of A1.

Gresley had visited Germany in 1933 and travelled on the twin articulated diesel electric 'Flying Hamburger' service between Berlin and Hamburg, which ran at an average speed over 77 mph and regularly achieved 100 mph. Gresley concluded that he could achieve a similar performance utilising one of his Pacifics and a lightweight train. He experimented with 4472 Flying Scotsman on 30th November 1934 hauling a 4-coach train, covering the 187 miles from King's Cross to Leeds at an average speed of 73 mph and officially recording 100 mph on the return journey. A similar journey with Class A3 'Papyrus' and a heavier train in March 1935 achieved a top speed of 108 mph. This proved to Gresley and the LNER management that a high-speed intercity service could be run from London to the North East with conventional coaches in four hours.

Gresley was encouraged by LNER General Manager Sir Ralph Wedgwood to apply streamlining (as was the fashion of the time) to his locomotive designs, as much for the publicity benefit as any aerodynamic efficiency. Gresley also applied some radical improvements to his Pacific design including a wedge-shaped nose and streamlined boiler casing, combined with an increased boiler pressure of 250 psi, larger combustion chamber and increased valve diameter. 35 of this new class of locomotive, the A4, were built from 1935 to 1938 at Doncaster and benefited from improvements in the design of the internal steam circuits by the smoothing of the pipework to ensure no loss of pressure. The first four locomotives were allocated to the new 4-hour streamlined London to Newcastle service, The Silver Jubilee, introduced in September 1935. The new

Plate 14 - Nigel Gresley

locomotives performed superbly from the off and on the inaugural run, pioneer of the class No 2509 'Silver Link' achieved a new speed record of $112\frac{1}{2}$ mph. The most noted Class A4 'Pacific' performance however, was achieved on Sunday 3rd July 1938. Newly delivered Class A4 No. 4468 'Mallard' whilst hauling a 'test' train of 240 tons down Stoke Bank, reached a maximum speed of 126 mph, thus attaining a world record for steam traction that still stands to this day. Whilst developing his Pacific locomotives, Gresley had also designed a wide range of other successful locomotive types for specific traffic duties on the LNER. This included the Class P1 and P2 2-8-2 'Mikado' types; the latter designed to haul 500-ton trains over the steeply graded Edinburgh to Aberdeen line. The first of these locomotives No 2001 'Cock of the North' delivered in 1934 and employing a double 'Kylchap' exhaust blast pipe was subject to exhaustive testing in France at the newly opening Vitry test plant. Five more locomotives of the class followed between 1934 and 1936, adopting from 1936 onwards the streamline nose end used on the Class A4.

In 1930 a well proportioned 2-6-2 3-cylinder tank engine, the Class V1 was introduced and in 1936 the first of a class of powerful freight engines the V2 2-6-2 'Green Arrow' was completed at the Plant, named after the new LNER guaranteed delivery high-speed freight service. Other designs included the N2 0-6-2 suburban tank engine, and K4 2-6-0's designed for the West Highland line. One of Gresley's final designs was the lightweight 2-6-2 locomotive, the Class V4, a scaled-down version of the Class V2 with nickel steel boiler, of which only two locomotives were completed due to the intervening war, the first being named 'Bantam Cock'. The second locomotive was fitted with a thermic siphon to aid water circulation in the boiler, the first application of its type to an LNER locomotive.

Just prior to the outbreak of the Second World War, Sir Nigel Gresley (knighted in 1937) and his design team were developing a new 0-4-4-0 (Bo-Bo) electric locomotive. This was intended for the new Manchester-Sheffield-Wath 1500

Plate 15 - Edward Thompson

Volt dc electrification scheme and was built at the Works between 1939 and 1941. Work on the route was suspended during the Second World War although the locomotive No 6701 underwent trials on the Manchester-Altringham suburban lines in 1941 before being placed in store until the end of hostilities. Gresley died on 5th April 1941 from heart failure and was succeeded as LNER Chief Mechanical Engineer by Edward Thompson (Plate 15), who had held various positions with the GNR, North Eastern Railway and LNER. His period of office mainly covered the War years when there was little opportunity for implementing new designs. The Plant itself was largely engaged in armaments work, and to meet an urgent need for a mixed traffic engine, 50 LMS Stanier-designed 2-8-0 Class 8F locomotives were erected between 1943-46. Thompson introduced a policy of standard locomotive designs for the LNER, which included rebuilding several of Gresley's engines in order to provide prototypes for new locomotive classes. This included the Class P2 2-8-2's, in a move that not only dismayed the Doncaster workforce, but also proved to be largely unsuccessful. At the same time, Thompson dispensed with Gresley's conjugated valve gear, which had proved troublesome to maintain particularly during the economies of the war years. Thompson's project that encountered the most criticism was however the rebuilding of Gresley's first Class A1 Pacific 'Great Northern'. The locomotive looked so different and ungainly on completion that Thompson was accused of blatant vindictiveness.

Thompson however did produce several designs that arguably may be considered as his own. These were the successful B1 4-6-0 (Antelope) class, L1 2-6-4 tank of which the prototype No 9000 was built at the Plant and the Class A2/3 Pacific. Four diesel electric shunters also appeared during Thompson's era, all being constructed at the Plant during 1944. They were based on the English Electric Co. LMS twin-motor design, but with minor detail

differences and were largely used in Whitemoor Yard at March, Cambridgeshire.

Thompson retired in 1946 and was succeeded by Arthur Henry Peppercorn (Plate 16), the last person to hold the LNER Chief Mechanical Engineer's post. Peppercorn, in contrast to Thompson, was a great admirer of Gresley's ideas and re-introduced several of his design characteristics. These appeared on his first Class A2 locomotive built at Doncaster in 1947, the last locomotive to be built at the Plant under the LNER. A further 14 of these engines and Peppercorn's new Class A1 Pacific design were completed at The Plant under the newly nationalised British Railways. Peppercorn retired in 1949 after producing only a small number of new locomotive classes. However, his Class A1 is often considered to be the most reliable and economic 'Pacific' ever built.

British Railways 1948-1968

Following nationalisation, individual locomotive works were controlled by R A Riddles, Member of the Railway Executive for Mechanical and Electrical Engineering. Under a new national locomotive policy, selected practices from each of the former railway companies were incorporated in designs for a new range of 12 'standard' steam locomotives. The

Plate 16 - Arthur Peppercorn

overall design emphasis was on ease of maintenance and simplicity of operation. Work on the projected 12 BR Standard designs commenced during 1949 and was divided between the drawing offices at Brighton, Derby, Doncaster, and Swindon. Complete locomotives were no longer designed by one Works, though each design office had the responsibility for overseeing the general arrangement drawings for one or more of the Standard Classes and for producing a standard drawing for a particular group of locomotive parts. Doncaster was responsible for coupling and connecting rods, valve gear and cylinder details.

Prior to building BR Standard Class locomotives at the Plant, a batch of Class 4F 2-6-0 engines were produced between 1950 and 1952. They were to the design of H G Ivatt (Henry Alfred Ivatt's son) for the LMS prior to nationalisation. Later, between 1952 to 1957, the Works constructed locomotives belonging to three Standard Class groups: the 2-6-0 Class 4, 4-6-0 Class 5 and the 2-6-4 Tank Engine. During 1957, Class 4 No 76114 was the last of 2,228 steam locomotives to be built at Doncaster, three years before steam locomotive construction ceased nationally.

A report by the British Transport Commission in 1955 had authorized the gradual withdrawal of steam locomotives in favour of diesel-electric, diesel-mechanical and electric traction. Under this new policy, one of the first building programmes the Works became involved in was the production of diesel shunting locomotives. Construction extended over the years 1957 to 1961 and included Classes 03 (82 locomotives) and 08 (30 locomotives). In 1959, the first main line electric locomotives since prototype No 6701 were manufactured at The Plant. These were 24 DC electric locomotives numbered E5000-5023 (later Class 71), built for the Southern Region's Kent Coast Electrification Scheme. Two years later the Works both designed and produced 40 AC electric locomotives, type AL5 (later Class 85). These were part of an order from the British Transport Commission for an initial 100 prototype AC main-line electric locomotives to work the 'West Coast' route from London Euston to Birmingham, Manchester and Liverpool. Following their success under varying traffic conditions a production version, the AL6 (Class 86), appeared in 1965/6 with 40 out of a batch of 100 being built at the Plant, numbered E3101 to E3140. Doncaster was the 'parent' design office for both the Class 85 and 86 locomotives.

British Rail Engineering Ltd (BREL) 1968-1987

The 1968 Transport Act enabled BR workshops to compete for work in other industries under the name of British Rail Engineering Limited (BREL). The Plant became a part of the group of BREL workshops and during 1970 collaborated with two private companies, Hunslet Engineering Company Ltd and English Electric AE1 Traction, to provide three locomotives for Northern Ireland Railways. In 1973 the Works won an order from London Transport to build 11 battery locomotives Nos L44-L54 completed in 1974. Two years later, work began on converting eight EMU motorcars Class 501 to battery-electric departmental locomotives (Nos 97703-97710) for BR electrification project work.

In the mid-1970s, BR placed an order with Romanian company Electropute to provide 30 Class 56 locomotives for heavy freight duties. Following completion, the locomotives were tested and underwent acceptance trials at The Plant, where it was discovered that they were of inferior quality and below acceptable British standards. The following 85 of the Class were built at the Plant, with body construction in the Fabrication Shop and assembly in the New Erecting Shop, with the last 20 locomotives manufactured at Crewe Works.

Shortly before Class 56 construction was transferred to Crewe, a development and building programme began at Doncaster on the Class 58 locomotive. This was designed as a cheaper alternative to the Class 56 based upon modular component parts bolted to a sturdy underframe. The first locomotive 58001 appeared from the Plant in December 1982 with the final member of the Class 58050 emerging

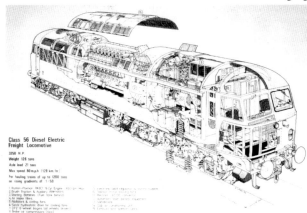

Plate 17 - Class 56 Locomotive

four years later. This was the last locomotive to be built by the Works under British Rail prior to a major restructuring programme. Throughout the BREL period Doncaster Works continued to be the sole BR workshop to carry out the regular maintenance of many locomotive types. This included Classes 03, 08, 13, 23, 31, 37, 55 Deltics and Class 76 electric locomotives. During the early 1970s a number of major modifications were undertaken on Class 83 and 84 electric locomotives.

During 1979, a substantial refurbishment programme was won by the Works comprising a five-year contract to completely overhaul and upgrade the Western Region Class 50 fleet of fifty locomotives. The work involved virtually rebuilding the locomotives from the frames upwards and with the exception of the power unit, refitting them with new equipment, including redesigning much out-of-date early electronic equipment from the 1960's. The Works also had responsibility for scrapping various locomotive types including Classes 03, 08, 13, 24, 25, 40, 45, 46 and 55. In some instances much equipment was 'cannibalised' from the locomotives prior to cutting up in order to keep others in service. Other important work for BREL included the manufacture and repair of container lifting frames in addition to the repair, overhaul and testing of mobile cranes, forklift trucks and lifting tackle. The Works also carried out much non-railway work for the private sector including building hay balers, earth moving equipment, bridges and ventilating ducts.

British Rail Maintenance Limited (BRML) 1987-1995

Following the establishment of the BRML 'Level 5' Depot at the Works in April 1987, this area became involved with the maintenance of many locomotive classes in service throughout the north of England, plus classified attention to new 'second generation' DMU's. Repairs were also undertaken on Class 08 shunters, Non-Passenger Coaching Stock and 'old generation' DMU's. The Depot's main function was to provide a cost-effective facility to British Rail, including component exchange, with the vehicle given a general inspection and a repaint, enabling a quick turnround to be achieved with a speedy return to traffic being the key requirement. The new Depot was largely based in the Crimpsall Repair Shop and dealt with locomotive Classes 08, 20, 37, 47, 56 and 58 in addition to DMU's and Non-Passenger Coaching Stock. Heavy General Repairs were also carried out on Class 31 locomotives for about the first year of the Depot's existence in a contract left over from BREL days. However, the Class 31s were the only locomotives on which Doncaster repaired components, continuing a long association with maintenance on this type of vehicle.

Cost effective maintenance or component change was not usually carried out on Class 08 shunter locomotives, since this type of work was generally done at 'Level 4' Depots or where the vehicle was based. However, Doncaster undertook tasks that could not be done at those locations including wheels, coupling rods, generators and power units. From the outset, Doncaster BRML Depot was the largest one of its type on BR and employed over 750 people. It quickly gained a high reputation for the its extensive facilities, quality of work and quick turnround of vehicles. This reputation resulted in Doncaster being awarded work from other Depots, including HST collision damage repairs from Neville Hill Depot at Leeds.

ABB (later Adtranz) 1995-2001 now Bombardier Transportation

Late in October 1995, following the recent privatisation of the BRML Depot, new owners ABB were celebrating the handover of the first 'Triplet Set' for use on European Night Services from the UK through the Channel Tunnel. A triplet set consisted of two modified Class 37/6 locomotives and a generator van converted from a Mark 3 Sleeper vehicle. Re-engineered by ABB, each Triplet Set was designed to haul European Night Stock sleeper vehicles when operating on non-electrified routes between London, Swansea and Plymouth with the generator set providing power for all on-board services.

The ABB/Adtranz (now Bombardier) side of Doncaster Works has maintained a close association with the 31 HSBC-owned Class 91 locomotives that operate on the East Coast main line for GNER. This has included the carrying out of 'Cost Effective Maintenance' repairs at both F and G exams. However, in 1999 the company was awarded a major contract not only to undertake the heavy maintenance requirements of the fleet but to carry out a series of improvements to the locomotives so that they could reasonably be expected to travel 25,000 miles without failure. This Heavy General Repair program has included a significant amount of modifications to the locomotives, including the adoption of a reliability-centred maintenance philosophy, and the overhaul of the entire electric traction system. The latter improvements were carried out by Alstom Transportation's facilities at Preston, prior to refitment to the locomotives at Doncaster. The benefits of these modifications are now being seen in an all-round improvement in vehicle reliability and performance.

In 2001 GNER awarded a contract to Bombardier Transportation Systems for the rewire and modification of their entire High Speed Train (HST) Power Car fleet. This work includes rewiring both the main power cables and auxiliary electrical systems giving much improved reliability for the operator GNER. Whilst each Power Car is out of service for this work a number of important safety

system modifications and other examination work is being encompassed at the same time.

RFS Industries 1987-1993, RFS (E) Limited 1994-2000 now Wabtec Rail Limited

An early acquisition of the newly formed RFS was that of the industrial locomotive manufacturer Thomas Hill of Kilnhurst, Rotherham in July 1989. This included shunting locomotives bearing the famous 'Sentinel' name, in addition to its range of 'Vanguard', 'Valiant' and 'Steelman' types. The Kilnhurst Works then became the focus for RFS' locomotive work, including the transfer of Class 08 work from Doncaster, dealing with up to 50 locomotives per year on overhaul and major repairs. At this time Thomas Hill were also delivering two 'Mantis' locomotives, fitted with 'Hiab'-type cranes for general infrastructure work, one to the Docklands Light Railway in London (equipped with third rail power collection) and one to the Manchester Metrolink tram system.

RFS were also successful in this period in winning locomotive work for the Channel Tunnel construction. This included 7 'Challenger' narrow gauge contractors' locomotives built at both Doncaster (in D Shop, the old Erecting Shop) and Kilnhurst, for Trans Manche Link for use during tunnelling operations. The company also supplied twenty Class 20 locomotives to CTTG (Channel Tunnel Trackwork Group). These locomotives, withdrawn by BR, were overhauled and brought back into service, fitted with catalytic converters for use on contractors' trains on Channel Tunnel trackwork construction.

In view of RFS' difficult trading position, the decision was taken in the summer of 1993, to close the Kilnhurst Works and relocate shunting locomotive work to Doncaster. As London Underground stock occupied the New Erecting Shop, shunters had to be accommodated rather unsatisfactorily for a time on one road within the Heavy Shop. Despite these difficulties, RFS was successful in winning a contract to supply a large shunting locomotive to Tilcon for use in their Swinden quarry site, near Grassington. Comprising a massive steel slab frame and bogies, the locomotive weighed in at 150 tonnes, at its time the heaviest locomotive of its kind in the UK, providing the necessary tractive effort required within the heavily graded quarry environment. The locomotive was constructed in the New Erecting Shop and was successfully completed through the difficult period of receivership in 1994. Because of its shear size the locomotive was delivered in three parts for assembly on the customer's site.

During 1997 RFS(E) were to win a major refurbishment contract with Direct Rail Services (DRS), the train operating company of British Nuclear Fuels Limited for the overhaul of six Class 20 locomotives. Using a variety of donor locomotives, including ex-RFS Channel Tunnel locomotives, an extensive scope of work was undertaken, including a complete strip down and rewire, major bodywork and cab replating and a range of modifications to update the locomotive systems and provide extra capabilities. These included long-range fuel tanks, a complete cab refurbishment, fire detection systems and modern cab communication equipment. The awarding of the contract saw the welcome return of mainline locomotive work to the New Erecting Shop. The locomotives were successfully completed to a tight deadline with the first locomotive, renumbered 20306, appearing in March 1998. On the strength of the work completed on the first six locomotives a further 4 locomotives were similarly refurbished for DRS between March and October 1998.

The company has maintained a significant presence in the Class 08 and industrial shunter overhaul and hire market. For the construction of the new Heathrow Express railway, RFS (E) supplied three 0-4-0 'Sentinel' locomotives adapted for tunnel work, to engineering consortium Laing Bailey in 1996 and 1997. Delivery to site required the locomotives to be vertically lowered into the tunnel section down a 100-feet deep ventilation shaft. In 1997 RFS(E) won a contract with GNER for the provision of Class 08's at their Bounds Green (London) and Craigentinny (Edinburgh) depots, with the locomotives carrying the characteristic GNER dark blue and orange stripe livery. Doncaster Works regularly undertakes work on EWS Class 08 locomotives that has included the installation of radio-control equipment to 5 locomotives, enabling them to remotely driven from the trackside. 2002 saw the completion of a General Overhaul programme to nine Class 08's belonging to passenger train operator First Great Western for their depots in London, South Wales and the South West.

Other mainline locomotive work has comprised the replacement of main bearings on Class 60 power units and the completion of 'cab quiet' modifications on Class 66 locomotives. The latter work required the stripping of driving cab insulation and its replacement with improved sound absorbing materials. An intensive programme of up to 13 locomotives per week was successfully undertaken for EWS, followed by Freightliner's Class 66 fleet. Class 20 work has continued with further locomotive overhauls and repairs for Michael Owen and DRS. Class 47 work has included bogie overhauls for Freightliner as part of the Class 57 conversion programme and overhaul and rewiring work for Cotswold Rail. 2003 has seen the arrival of Network Rail's (formerly Railtrack) fleet of Multi Purpose Vehicles for annual examination work, and HST Power Cars for modification as part of Network Rail's New Measurement Train. With an extensive modern paint facility a number of mainline locomotives have received reliverying in recent years including Class 90002 'Mission Impossible' for the launch of Virgin Train's West Coast franchise, EWS and Hanson Class 59's, DRS Class 20 and 37's and Cotswold Rail 47's.

4 Carriage, Wagon and Multiple Unit Work

1853 to 1905

Shortly before the GNR. transferred its Works from Boston to Doncaster in 1853, John Coffin was appointed as the Company's Inspector of Rolling Stock. When the move was completed Coffin became the Works' first Carriage Superintendent. It is not clear whether Coffin ever designed carriages himself, but under his guidance, carriage construction began at Doncaster some time after the mid-1850's, preceding that of locomotives by at least ten years. After a relatively short working life at the Plant, Coffin died in April 1858 and was replaced by John Griffiths, who was a coach-builder by trade. With the latter in charge in the early 1860s, the Works began

constructing vehicles for the East Coast Joint Stock, as well as meeting the GNR's own carriage needs. The ECJS was the term used for carriages especially intended for the Anglo-Scottish (London-Edinburgh) services. The cost of building and maintaining these carriages was jointly provided by the GNR, North Eastern Railway and North British Rail over whose territory the route extended. The first ECJS service began in 1861, with a large proportion of the carriages used, being built at Doncaster (until the turn of the century) and by private contractors.

Throughout the latter half of the 19th century the latest features in carriage design were usually fitted to the ECJS before being introduced to other vehicles owned by the three constituent companies. However, Plant produced vehicles for the ECJS and the GNR in the 1850s and 60s were austere, lacking both style and facilities. First Class carriages and compartments were more comfortable than Second, Third or Fourth Class, but one of the more frightening features of all carriages was the primitive brakes. As power brakes were not introduced until late in the century, the trains had to rely on the locomotive's brakes or those fitted to 'brake' coaches. These usually had 'brakesmen' seated high up on them to see signal stops and then apply the brakes. For an emergency stop the locomotive drives had to attract the brakesman's attention by using a whistle signal from the engine.

Rail travel was improved during the 1870s in America by the type of carriages and services offered by George Pullman. This included the introduction of the Sleeping Car, which made the passengers' journey more comfortable and was an immediate success. Several of Pullman's ideas were adopted in England including the Sleeping Car, and in 1873 the Works produced a similar vehicle for the ECJS one of the first to be built in this country. Pullman's vehicles were also fitted with bogies (pivoted trucks at each end of the carriage) to give the passenger a more comfortable ride than the standard British carriage of this period, which had four or six 'rigid' wheels. Consequently, in 1875, The Plant introduced its first bogie vehicles. Natural day-time lighting in carriages was improved during the mid-1870s by the introduction of the clerestory roof. Safety was also enhanced by the adoption of vacuum brakes in 1879. A number of GNR and East Coast carriages emerging from The Plant around this period featured these developments.

Earlier, in 1876 John Griffiths retired and his post as Carriage & Wagon Superintendent was taken by EF Howlden. In 1882 the latter had the honour of being authorised to build at Doncaster the first British side-gallery or corridor carriage, which was intended for the ECJS. The corridor ran the full length of the vehicle, giving access to toilet facilities at each end. Prior to this toilets were only provided in First Class vehicles or, to a limited extent, in small compartments between the passenger compartments. The new vehicle, however, did not have 'end' doors or 'bellows' to allow passenger movement into adjoining vehicles.

In the early 1890s there was a general acceptance of Dining Cars, large corridor carriages mounted on four or six-wheeled bogies, Gould centre couplers, 'bellows' gangways and connecting doors. An example of the type of Plant vehicles being produced at this time were the four Third Class, dining Cars which were built in 1894 for the ECJS service the 'Day Scotsman'. The cars had square-ended vestibules and a clerestory roof, running the whole length of the vehicle. Gangway connections, for passage to adjoining coaches, were at the side not the centre. Passengers were accommodated in three separate saloons with a total of 42 seats. Three ECJS sets built later in the decade at The Plant were fitted with a short Pullman gangway. The latter feature was considered to be much safer and stronger for passenger movement between vehicles than the long, Gould 'bellows' gangway. All gangway connections on the carriages were located centrally. During 1899 HA Ivatt led a party of railway officials to the United States to investigate the use of automatic couplers. As a result the buckeye automatic coupler began to replace Gould's coupler on subsequent GNR and ECJS vehicles.

In 1900 The Plant built for the ECJS, three Composite First/Third Dining Saloons with central kitchens as well as three First Class Dining Cars with their own kitchens. Some of these were used for the first time with the 'Flying Scotsman' service and standard features on ECJS built in 1899-1900 comprised clerestory roofs and Pullman vestibules. The Works also introduced these features on the GNR main-line vehicles particularly those working the Leeds-King's Cross services. The turn of the century also saw the introduction of steam-heating replacing more primitive heating methods like footwarmers and oil stoves. In 1902 some of the first carriages with steel underframes were built at Doncaster. These were initially used on secondary trains to Manchester. EF Howlden retired as The Plant's Carriage & Wagon Superintendent in 1905. He had started his career in the carriage department during the 1850s when it was commonplace to see crude four-wheeled, main-line vehicles. At the time of his retirement, carriages had continuous brakes, steam heating, electric lighting and excellent toilet and refreshment facilities.

1905 to 1941

Nigel Gresley was appointed as Carriage & Wagon Superintendent shortly after Howlden's retirement. His initial carriage designs were for the vehicles attached to Ivatt's railmotors numbered 1 and 2, which appeared from the Plant in 1905. One of the main features of these carriages was the elliptical roof, which Gresley argued was stronger, lighter and provided better ventilation than a clerestory roof. From 1905 elliptical roofs were adopted as standard for the ECJS Other developments, in contemporary carriage design included all new GNR bogie stock being fitted with electric lighting and a move towards all steel underframes. Gresley improved the riding of certain carriages by making adjustments to the springs and suspension. Vibration and running noise was also reduced by placing India-rubber 'cushions' between floors and underframes.

The first Gresley-designed train sets were introduced in 1906 for services between King's Cross-Sheffield and Manchester and became known as the 'Sheffield Stock'. The group of carriages earned Gresley praise from the GNR since they provided a higher standard of passenger comfort than had previously been achieved. A year later, Gresley was asked to improve the riding of

the old Howlden six-wheeled ECJS, which was still operating on some services between King's Cross and Edinburgh. The easiest solution would have been to replace the old vehicles entirely, but as the North Eastern Railway was unable to make any financial contribution Gresley decided that passenger comfort could be increased if these carriages were mounted on articulated bogies. The result was successful and further units of two, three, four and five carriages were joined together. In 1911 immediately before Gresley became Locomotive Superintendent he introduced a 'high' elliptical roofed carriage for secondary duties, new stock for London suburban trains and double bolster bogies. The last feature was gradually adopted as standard for all main-line passenger stock.

Edward Thompson succeeded Gresley, though the latter continued to keep a watchful eye on carriage development. During the three years before the First World War, carriage-building activities at the Works concentrated on the production of new articulated suburban sets, alongside the further articulation of Howlden's non-bogie stock. By 1914, non-bogie stock was converted into 99 twin-bodied sets, 13 triple-bodied sets, 18 quadruple sets and one quintuple set of five coach bodies mounted on six bogies. In the same year a new 'Flying Scotsman' train for East Coast services was built at Doncaster, and electricity replaced gas on all main-line express stock, except for Kitchen Cars, following a Board of Trade recommendation.

The First World War resulted in Thompson temporarily leaving Doncaster in 1916 to help at the Woolwich Aresnal. Later he served in France and attained the rank of Lieutenant-Colonel. During the 1914-18 period, articulation work and building of new vehicles virtually ceased, as the Works became more involved with the war effort. Thompson was demobilized in 1919, though his return to Doncaster was only brief, since he resigned from his post a year later. His successor was OVS Bulleid, who immediately established a good working relationship with Gresley. This was in complete contrast to Thompson, who had always quarrelled with Gresley. Under the first two years of Bulleid's supervision, The Plant produced a quintuple set of carriages for the London-Leeds services and a twin articulated Sleeping Car for the ECJS The London-Leeds set, built in 1921 included a Kitchen Car, which for the first time in England contained electric cooking equipment.

Following Gresley's 1923 appointment as Chief Mechanical Engineer of the newly formed LNER he moved from Doncaster to an office at King's Cross with Bulleid as his personal assistant and several other Plant staff including Bert Spencer, Frank Day and Norman Newsome. The connection between King's Cross and The Plant, where Francis Wintour was left in overall change, was very strong. All new design work after its initial conception at King's Cross was carried out in The Plant drawing office, with small detailed designs being delegated to other LNER drawing offices. One of the first schemes the King's Cross/Doncaster teams were occupied with was the introduction of standardised non-corridor and corridor stock. During the 1920s and 30s the Plant was heavily involved with constructing the various types of standard corridor carriages, including: First Side Corridors, Brake First Corridors and First Open Corridors. Apart from building a batch of quadruple-articulated non-corridor stock in 1924, the Works was less committed to the non-corridor vehicle.

The introduction in 1928 of the first non-stop 'Flying Scotsman' service was one of the great events in railway history. For the service, a new set of carriages was constructed and part of The Plant's work involved producing Restaurant Car triplet sets. Gresley took a personal interest in the vehicles' internal decor and asked his friend Sir Charles Allom, a furnishing specialist, to produce ideas for them. As a result the vehicles were decorated in a Louis XIV style, which was a decisive break with the earlier Edwardian styles.

The following decade marked a period of instability in the field of carriage construction, since rail travel became increasingly threatened by the developments in road transport. LNER carriage construction actually ceased for a short time in 1932, but by 1938 had reached maximum output again. New practices included in the Company's 1930s carriage building programme were the introduction of pressure ventilation (1930), an all-welded underframe (1934) and steel panel coaches (1935). Despite the instability of the 1930s the decade heralded the Works' finest achievements in carriage design and production, as Doncaster was chosen by the LNER to build high-speed train sets. The Company's other carriage building centre at York and Dukinfield were, left to concentrate on general service corridor and non-corridor coaches. In 1935 the design sections of the Cowlairs, Darlington, Gorton and Stratford drawing offices were closed and all LNER design work took place at Doncaster. In the same year the Plant produced its first 'streamline' train the 'Silver Jubilee' set to operate a service between King's Cross and Newcastle. Each set of carriages comprised seven vehicles, two articulated twins and a Restaurant/Kitchen Car triplet, and was largely intended to cater for businessmen on their journeys to and from the capital. All the vehicles had steel body panels and were covered externally in silver-grey rexine with stainless steel trim. The rexine, however, did not withstand wear and tear and the carriages were eventually sprayed silver. Despite this the 'Jubilee' set was an immediate success with passengers proving itself commercially, as well as earning the LNER a considerable amount of prestige. Two years later the Works built the London-Edinburgh 'Coronation' train sets, which were introduced to coincide with the 1937 Coronation celebrations of King George VI. Another prestigious group of Plant-built carriages, which appeared in 1937 was the 'West Riding Limited' set. These were intended to operate on the Bradford-Leeds-King's Cross service. There was, however, a change in fortune for The Plant's carriage building department at the outset of the 1940s. The Main Carriage Building Shop was destroyed by an accidental fire on 21st December 1940, and four months later, Sir Nigel Gresley, the person responsible for many of the famous Doncaster-built carriages, was dead.

1941 to 1968

When Edward Thompson became LNER Chief Mechanical Engineer in 1941, he had been appointed for the second time in his career, to a position formerly occupied by Gresley. Coincidentally on both occasions, war intervened and severely restricted Thompson's plans and policies. In addition, until the fire-damaged Main Carriage Shop was rebuilt, Plant carriage construction was only minimal. In spite of these external pressures, Thompson produced designs for new standard stock and two prototype vehicles emerged from the Works around 1944-45. General production of the vehicles began in 1946, the same year as Thompson retired. A H Peppercorn, who succeeded Thompson, made little, if any, impression on carriage design, although his activities were restricted by the imminence of nationalisation. The Works' new Main Carriage Shop was completed in 1949 and several carriages for a new 'Flying Scotsman' set were amongst the first vehicles to be built there. These included a Buffet Lounge and a Kitchen Car. A year later Peppercorn retired.

After the inception of British Railways in 1948, R A Riddles, the Mechanical & Electrical Engineering member of the Railway Executive, established a Carriage Standards Committee, which consisted of senior carriage and wagon department draughtsmen from each of the former main-line railway companies. Consequently several far-reaching decisions about carriage design and construction were made. It was decided that new carriages would be of a 'standard' format, rather than perpetuate any of the existing 'company' styles. However, the more salient features of the four main-line companies were included. Externally and to some extent internally the carriages resembled both the LMS and the last Southern Railway vehicles. LNER features included buckeye automatic couplers on corridor coaches and Pullman style gangways. The Carriage Standards Committee produced the drawings for the main design features and then allocated detail design of each vehicle type to one of the regional design offices. In addition the new vehicles had to be compatible with all existing stock and capable of operating over the whole railway system.

As there was a scarcity of good timber during the post-war years, the body frame was made of steel instead of wood. Steel also had the advantages of being lighter and stronger. However, if a steel body was to be used, a choice had to be made between the traditional method (of building a body on to separate load bearing underframe) and an integral construction (where the body was designed to take some of the loading strasses and the underframe is lighter but not an independent unit). In the event, the former was adopted after both alternatives had been subjected of the loading stresses and the underframe is lighter-but not an independent to rigorous analysis. Primarily, this was made because a carriage underframe was estimated to last 40 years almost twice as long as a body, which was more prone to corrosion. Consequently, it was a more viable proposition to replace the carriage unit on the more durable underframe than build a completely new vehicle. Many of the new standard or Mark 1 vehicles, as they became known, were not built as an entire unit at one BR Works. For example, York provided underframes for a number of coaches completed at Doncaster. The Plant's first Mark 1 vehicle, a Kitchen Car, emerged during 1951. Over the next seven years other vehicles produced were: First Restaurant Cars,

Second Sleepers, Open Firsts, Open Seconds, Open Brakes, Corridor Seconds, Composites, Second Opens and General Utility Vans. Diesel Multiple Units, although in use during the early 1950s, became more widely employed after the 1955 Modernisation Programme. Although no DMUs were built at Doncaster, repairs were carried out there on the many different types. However, The Plant did not undertake heavy repairs on the underfloor diesel engines, this being allocated to other B.R. Works.

In 1957, BR ordered from its own workshops and private contractors 14 prototype carriages. The remit was to experiment with coach design and layout within the limitations of the standard underframe and an all steel body shell. The Plant built six of these carriages, including an Open First, Open Second, Corridor First and Corridor Second. Disappointingly all 14 prototype vehicles were not a great improvement on existing stock and provided little direct influence on subsequent vehicle construction. Doncaster completed its programme of Mark 1 carriage construction in 1958 with a Second Class Sleeping Car. A year later the Works began production on 112 four-car sets of electric stock (Class 302) for use on the Fenchurch Street lines in London. Doncaster built the bodies, whilst York Carriage Works and the English Electric Company respectively provided the bogies and power equipment. A further 14 four-sets of EMU stock (Class 305/2) emerged from the Works during 1960-61 for use on the Liverpool Street to Herford East and Bishop's Stortford lines. Construction details followed a similar pattern to the previous sets. A year later, a passenger vehicle was converted at Doncaster to an instrument Coach for testing overhead equipment on electrified routes. The unit was part of a two car set the other vehicle being an Observation Coach.

After the 1962 BR Workshops Re-organisation Plan was implemented, carriage building and repairs, excluding DMUs ceased at Doncaster. The EMUs had been the last large carriage construction order completed at the Plant and the last official repair was in 1964. During 1964-65 the Main Carriage Shop was vacated, being subsequently reorganised as a Wagon Heavy Repair Shop, to undertake work which had been removed from the Carr Wagon Works.

BREL 1968-1987

In 1971 coach work made a brief return to the Plant when the area assisted York Carriage Works to modernize around 70 Sleeping Cars. This was because York was already working to capacity. The work at Doncaster concerned around 35 vehicles and was carried out in the West Carriage Shop. Similarly in 1982 Doncaster assisted York to modernize about 70 Tourist Second Open vehicles by taking half the workload. On this occasion the work was undertaken in the Wagon Heavy Repair Shop (formerly the Main Carriage Shop). During the BREL years Doncaster was responsible for the maintenance, on average, of around 20 DMU vehicles a week as well as a vast number of Non Passenger Carrying Coaching Stock, conversions and classified overhauls.

Much wagon work also took place during this period with around 25 vehicles per week being repaired.

During 1977-78 a number of 'Presflo' wagons were refurbished under contract from the Associated Portland Cement Company Ltd. In the early 1980s, following the closure of Shildon Wagon Works, the Plant's involvement increased with the maintenance of the 32 ton, High Capacity, 'Merry-Go-Round', Coal Hopper Wagons. New wagon construction work included building several batches of vehicles for various customers. There were also overseas orders, the first of these occurred in 1984 and was from the L'office Du Chemin de Fer, Trans Gabonais, in Africa-for a dozen log-carrying bogie wagons.

BRML, 1987-1995, ABB (later Adtranz) 1995-2001 now Bombardier Transportation.

After the removal of DMU repairs from the West Carriage Shop, North Shed and other smaller 'satellite' buildings in 1986, the work was subsequently housed in three bays of the Crimpsall Repair Shop, where cost-effective maintenance and component change took place. For a time, 1, 1 A and 2 Bays accommodated DMU and National Passenger Carrying Coaching Stock (NPCCS) repairs. Two roads led into 1-bay where quick bogie changes took place at one end and DMU bogie repairs at the other. 1A-bay dealt with the repairs to various small components and 2-bay handled the main body repairs and repainting.

The Depot undertook classified repairs on 'old' generation DMUs as well as some component repairs. On NPCCS components were changed, bogies renovated and the body-work re-painted. In April 1988 began work on the 'new' generation Class 150 DMU's. Each Tuesday evening at 7.30 the Depot received a two-car set for C4 overhaul and during the night the bogies were changed, various components examined and replaced, and the vehicle returned to traffic the following morning. From August 1988 the Depot was receiving 2-car sets on Tuesday and Thursday evenings each week for component changes C4 overhaul.

From 1995 onwards under the ownership of ABB then Adtranz, the philosophy of the site changed from being an all-encompassing repair centre to one which concentrated purely upon vehicle repairs. This allowed major components to be dealt with at Doncaster on a unit-exchange basis with, for example, power units, traction motors, bogies, couplers and valves being sent to Adtranz's repair centre at Crewe Works. This generated more space on the site to accept rail vehicles including 23 sets of Class 365 EMU's from York during

Plate 18 - Name Change as ABB purchases Doncaster BRML Level 5 Depot in 1995

closure of the Works site. Later, the Works also saw the return of Class 156 and also Class 153 DMU's from Derby for C6 Classified Repairs and interior enhancements.

Under Adtranz and now Bombardier's ownership, the site has maintained a regular program of overhauls and enhancements to DMU fleets owned by Angel Trains. This has included C4 Classified Repairs (on an approximate 30-month periodicity) and a more extensive C6 repair usually carried out every 6 years. Vehicle reliverying and other interior enhancements, including new seating and carpets, have often been carried out in conjunction with the C6 Repair. This work has encompassed Class 142 Pacer units operated by Arriva and First North Western, Class 150 Sprinter units (Central Trains and First North Western), Arriva Class 153 & 156 units, and Class 158's (Central Trains and Wales & Borders).

RFS Industries 1987-1993, RFS (E) Limited 1994-2000 now Wabtec Rail Limited

At the inception of RFS the company was engaged in the manufacture of 124 wagons for English China Clay and a 3-year contract for the overhaul and repair of many types of BR wagon. This was in addition to a programme to rebody 200 'Merry-Go-Round' coal hoppers, fit new doors and undertake General Repairs to the running gear. Other private owner work undertaken in the early 1990's included ICI Methanol tank wagons and General Repairs on MOD 'Warwell' flat wagons. In addition to the supply of locomotives for Channel Tunnel construction work, RFS designed and manufactured two Channel Tunnel Bogie Test vehicles for Trans Manche Link in 1989. The early days of RFS were also to see a number of successful new wagon designs emerge from Doncaster. This included 12 prototype Railfreight Metals covered steel carriers (13, 16 and 19m long) with retractable hoods, capable of operation both in the UK and Europe and 265 90-tonne aggregate hoppers for RMC in 1990 to 1991.

In March 1988, RFS was successful in winning a major BRB contract to carry out Voith gearbox conversions to 50 2-car 'Pacer' Class 142/143 DMU's for the Provincial sector of BR. The Special Rail Products division of RFS designed and manufactured modern bogies for Class 323 and 465 'Networker' EMU's at a separate facility in Hexthorpe, Doncaster. This included the B5000 advanced suburban bogie, with the prototypes being manufactured in D Shop.

1990 saw the inception of RFS' 'Fleetcare' division with contracts for the fleet maintenance of RMC and NACCO wagons. The company has since established a significant presence in the field of maintenance of wagon fleets at customers' sites. Managed from Doncaster Works, with manned and mobile sites throughout the UK, the company is able to offer a comprehensive fleet management service, backed up by the significant resources and capabilities available at Doncaster. Current customers include Network Rails National Logistics Unit fleet of HOBS and Side Tipper ballast vehicles, vehicle lessors such as GE Capital and aggregate companies including Lafarge and RMC.

Plate 19 - Entrances to NSC and RFS

In 1992-1993 RFS' wagon work included General Repairs to Shell 2-axle and 100-ton petrol tankers and conversion of VCA/VDA vans. The latter conversion included the removal of the vehicle bodysides, retention of the end bulkheads and the fitting of vertical stanchions to make OTA timber carriers. At this time the first conversions of vans to 'Sea Urchin' box bodies were also carried out for BR. The advent of the BR freight companies prior to privatisation brought a number of contracts to Doncaster. These included further 'Sea Urchin' conversions for Mainline Freight and Transrail, the General Repair of 100t steel carriers and HEA hopper rebodying for Loadhaul. Private owner work at this time included the General Repair of BNFL FNA, PFA and 150 tonne PIA wagons, the conversion of 102 tonne Croxton & Garry cement powder wagons to carry slurry and the body strengthening of ECC china clay hoppers.

Diversification away from a sole reliance on BR led RFS to take on a major refurbishment contract for London Underground (LUL) 'C' stock in 1989. This included the manufacture of new bogies, and a significant degree of internal refurbishment. The original aluminium vehicle bodywork was painted in a smart red, white and blue livery. As a follow on to the 'C' Stock work, RFS entered into a further LUL contract to refurbish 1973 Piccadilly Line tube stock, but this foundered as a result of the company's poor trading position and receivership followed in December 1993. With the sale of the passenger side of the business to Bombardier ProRail in 1994, the residual part of this contract was completed at their Horbury Works near Wakefield.

Despite the loss of existing passenger contracts during receivership, the management of the reborn RFS(E) was eager to re-establish a passenger vehicle presence at Doncaster Works. The first passenger contract to be won was in 1995 for 38 2-car Class 156 DMU's, including the replacement of corroded roof sections and repainting, coordinated with an associated C6 overhaul programme by Adtranz in their adjacent facilities at the Crimpsall. Between 1998 and 2000 RFS(E) established a regular programme of Porterbrook Class 158 DMU work, including C6 overhauls, corrosion repairs and repainting for operators Northern Spirit, First North Western and Virgin Trains. The Works has also overhauled and repainted 12 Class 153 single car DMU's for First North Western in 2000. Passenger coach work has included 29 C4 and C6 overhauls from 1997 to 1999 on Mark 1 & 2A passenger coaches for Eversholt Leasing (now HSBC

Rail) and North Western Trains. The General Repair of ex-Mark 1 coaches converted to Railtrack Breakdown Vehicles was undertaken between 1997 and 1998. RFS(E) has also modified and reliveried barrier vehicles for Mark 4 vehicles in 2000, including repainting in GNER livery. The Works has undertaken a number of collision damage repairs including Class 142 and 156 DMU's and more recently a Class 333 EMU for Siemens and Arriva Trains Northern. C6 overhauls are currently being executed on 39 2-car Angel Trains' owned Class 158 DMU's for Wales & Borders and Wessex Trains. 2003 has seen the recommencement of C6 overhauls on Porterbrook Class 156 DMU's and the modification and reliverying of the high-speed track recording coach for use in Network Rail's New Measurement Train.

To support vehicles and bogie-based work at Doncaster and to support customer requirements in the field, the Works has maintained a growing component overhaul business including a large range of air brake equipment, including distributors, brake cylinders and actuators, load valves and slack adjusters, providing a number of customers with 'vehicle kits' of equipment to support their internal overhaul programmes at running depots. In 1998 Wabtec Rail entered the buffer overhaul market and provides EWS with a large variety of buffer types. The Works' damper overhaul business is one of the largest in the UK, and provides complete vehicle kits of dampers to many depots across the UK to support C4-type overhaul programmes.

Other wagon work for EWS has encompassed a series of major wagon conversions of various types over the last seven years. Over 500 redundant HAA coal wagons have had their hopper bodies removed and replaced by box bodies (reclassified as MHA), 220 TTA oil tankers have been converted to low sided boxes (MTA) as have HEA hoppers to MEA boxes. Private owner wagon work has included the conversion for Tiphook Rail (now GE Capital) in 1995 of 102-tonne curtain-sided steel coil carrying wagons to JXA boxes. This included the fitting of a high strength box for carrying scrap steel, with massively reinforced vehicle ends to cope with impact damage from electro-magnet unloading.

In autumn 1997 RFS(E) commenced the overhaul and standardisation of 22 Railtrack independent drift snowploughs. These vehicles were converted to snowploughs in the late 1950's and early 1960's from LNER 4200 gallon steam locomotive tenders. Extensive bodywork corrosion repairs were undertaken, and the original plain white metal bearings were replaced by roller bearings and the vacuum brake equipment by modern air brakes. Two novel features incorporated into the refurbished vehicles included a special vehicle coupler for towing ploughs blade-to-blade and a roof-mounted icicle breaker.

In 1999 the company was engaged by Jarvis Rail to design and manufacture 32 KRA sleeper-carrying wagons to work with a Track Renewal Train (TRT) under construction by Fairmont in South Carolina, USA. The TRT removes old sleepers as it passes over them and replaces them with new sleepers carried on the wagons. Special gantry cranes run on rails mounted on the wagon frames to convey sleepers to and from the TRT. Sliding 'bridging' rails between wagons provide a continuous track on which the gantry cranes run. Following the success of the sleeper carrying wagons a further order was completed for 6 wagons for Harsco in 2001 to be deployed on the renewal of Northern Ireland Railway's (NIR) trackwork, including the provision of 5' 3" gauge bogies for operation on the NIR infrastructure.

In 1995 RFS(E), in conjunction with Tiphook Rail, developed a prototype ballast laying vehicle utilising surplus 90 tonne aggregate hopper wagons. Replacing the existing bottom discharge doors with 4 sets of modular 'gates' operated by radio control, ballast can be delivered accurately between the rails or outside of the rails on each side of the vehicle. One operator can typically control five vehicles at once by a hand-held radio controller; this high productivity system replacing older vehicles which manual screw-operated doors. The first wagon was converted in December 1995, shortly followed by a further nine vehicles in early 1996. Initially operated by freight operator Transrail, the vehicles fell into disuse during the early stages of railway privatisation. With the foresight of infrastructure company GTRM, the concept was revised and a further ten vehicles were converted in 1999, including the addition of a diesel-alternator on every fifth vehicle providing hydraulic power for the doors and external lighting. In total 104 vehicles have since been converted operating as part of Network Rail's National Logistic Unit fleet.

Following on from the conversion programme Wabtec Rail received an order in December 1999 for the new manufacture of 190 HOBS (High Output Ballast System) vehicles. Visually similar to the earlier conversions, they employ a 'track-friendly' Axle Motion 3 Bogie in place of the conventional Y25 bogie on the converted vehicles. Bodies were supplied by original manufacturer Arbel Fauvet Rail in France, with bogies assembled in the Czech Republic, with door gear from Trinity Industries in Romania. Final assembly was undertaken at Doncaster Works, including all pneumatic, hydraulic and electrical systems, fitting the diesel alternator sets, couplers, bogies and final painting. This pan-European approach ensured that vehicles were manufactured to the original equipment designs to meet Railtrack's delivery schedule of eight vehicles per week. During 2003 Wabtec Rail will be manufacturing a further fifty HOBS vehicles for Network Rail.

1998 saw the establishment of Wabtec Rail's passenger bogie overhaul business, with franchise length contracts awarded for the C4 overhaul of Class 15X and 158 DMU bogies for Central Trains (now Maintrain). Without access to the national float of bogie frames, the company successfully established a new industry benchmark 48-hour door-to-door overhaul. Subsequent growth in bogie business has seen the first overhauls of Class 323 ac EMU bogies for Maintrain, with bogies currently returning to Doncaster for their second round of overhauls, and the first overhauls of Class 325 Postal EMU's for EWS. Wabtec Rail's bogie projects have seen the 'stretching' of HST-type BT10 bogie frames and wheelsets to 5' 3" gauge for use on an Irish Rail Snack Car. More recently the Works has been undertaking overhauls of Class 158 bogies for Railpart and Turbostar DMU bogies for Maintrain, and work on Siemens Heathrow Express Class 332 bogies and wheelsets.

Bibliography

Anon. (1961) Multiple Unit Stock for New Great Eastern Electric Services. *The Railway Magazine* January.

Anon. (1970) 'Eagle' Leaves the Nest. *The Railway Magazine*, July.

Anon. (1970) Pull-and-Push 'Enterprise'. *The Railway Magazine*, September.

Anon. (1974) B.R.-Built locomotives for London Transport. *The Railway Magazine*, April.

Anon. (1986) Doncaster Works, The Changing Scene, *Rail Enthusiast* No. 54, March.

Armstrong. J. (1974) L.N.E.R. *Locomotive Development between 1911 and 1947*, Devon.

Brown, F.A.S. (1961) *Nigel Gresley Locomotive Engineer*, London.

Brown, F.A.S. (1966) *Great Northern Locomotive Engineers Vol.1 1846-1881*, London.

Brown, F.A.S. (1974) *From Stirling to Gresley 1882-1922*, Oxford.

Day, J.E. (1953) *Doncaster Plant Works*, Unpublished (Copy held in Doncaster Central Library, Reference Section).

Fry, E.V. (ed.) (1970) *Locomotives of the L.N.E.R. Part 2A, Tender Engines – Classes A1 to A10*, R.C.T.S.

Fry, E.V. (ed.) (1973) *Locomotives of the L.N.E.R. Part 2B, Tender Engines – Classes B1 to B19*, R.C.T.S.

Fry, E.V. (ed.) (1979) *Locomotives of the L.N.E.R. Part 3A, Tender Engines – Classes C1 to C11*, R.C.T.S.

Hardy, B. (1976) *London Underground Rolling Stock*, Middlesex.

Haresnape, B. (1977) *Ivatt and Riddles Locomotives: A Pictorial History*, Surrey.

Haresnape, B. (1983) *British Rail Fleet Survey No.6: Electric Locomotives*, Surrey.

Haresnape, B. (1983) *British Rail Fleet Survey No.8: Diesel Multiple Units*, Surrey.

Harris, M. (1973) *Gresley's Coaches*, Newton Abbott.

Kichenside, G.M. (1964) Thompson L.N.E.R. Post-War All- Steel Coaches-some Notes and Details. *Model Railway Constructor*, April.

Marsden, C.J. (1982) *Motive Power Recognition: 2.E.M.Us*, London.

Marsden, C.J. (1982)*35 Years of Main-Line Diesel Traction*, Oxford.

Marsden, C.J. (1983) *Rolling Stock Recognition-: Coaching Stock*, London.

Marsden, C.J. (1984) *Locomotive Numbering*, London.

Morrison, B. (1982) *The Power of the A4s*, Oxford.

Nock, O.S. (1945) *The Locomotives of Sir Nigel Gresley*, London.

Parkin, K. (1982) *Locomotive Hauled Mark 1 Coaching Stock of British Railways*, Somerset.

Talbot, E. (1982) *A Pictorial Record of British Railways Standard Steam Locomotives*, Oxford.

Weight, R.A.H. (1947) *Great Northern Locomotives 1847-1947*, Hastings.

Whiteley, J.S. and G.W. Morrison (1982) *The Power of the A1s, A2s and A3s*, Oxford.

Wild, L. (1984) *British Rail Freight Stock Part 1: Air Braked Hopper Vehicles*, Doncaster.

Wrottesley, J. (1979-1981) *The Great Northern Railway*, London.

Acknowledgements

We would like to thank Hugh Parkin, who first suggested the idea of a book about Doncaster Plant Works, for strong encouragement and assistance throughout the course of the project.

Gratitude should also be expressed to the following people: Philip Atkins, Nev Atkinson, Bill Baxter, Richard Bell, Terry Berner, Eric Braim, Mark Brennan, Doug Brown, Paul Buckland, Audrey Buttery, Miriam Burrell, Mick Carroll, Malcoilm Crawley, John Cuttriss, J. E. Day, Bernard Dixon, Edwin Dixon, Malcolm Dolby, Chris Duffell, Tony Vernon-Harcourt, Fastline Photographic, Jim Firth, Mike Gilbert, Geoff Goslin, V. Graves, Geoff Harrison, Terry Henderson, Peter Holmes, Dr Geoffrey Hughes, Philip Langford, John Law, Martin Limbert, David Livesey, Bob Machin, Colin Marsden, Eric Marshall, Chris Palmer, Noel Pantry, Arthur Pinkey, Derek Porter, Martin Porter, Bill Reed, R. Scott, Steve Skeldon (Railpart), Alan Smith and Neil Harvey (Bombardier Transportation Services), Peter Skidmore and Geoff Thomas, The Gresley Society.

Also a special thank you go to Ed Bartholomew and Jon Ingham of the National Rail Museum for the supply of images for use in this publication.

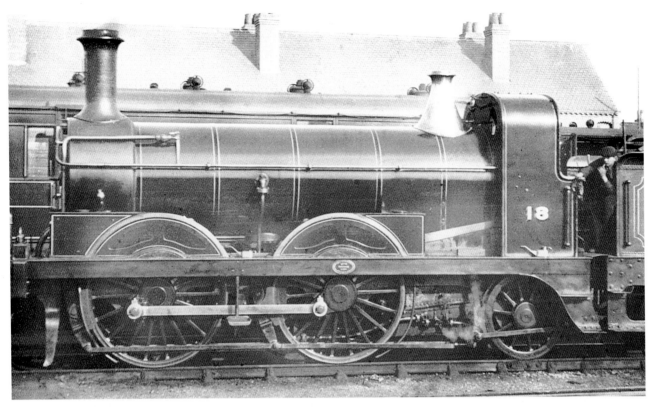

Doncaster's First Locomotive – The era of locomotive construction at Doncaster began in 1867 when 0-4-2, C class F2, No 18, emerged from the Plant bearing Works' plate No.1. The F2 was designed by Patrick Stirling as a 'mixed traffic' locomotive and 104 were built at Doncaster between 1867-1895. A further 50 were constructed by outside contractors making the total number of F2s built to 154. No. 18 is pictured here in its later modified form where the original 'porthole' cab had been replaced by a standard Stirling type.

Prince of Wales Saloon – Following a complaint by the Prince of Wales in August 1875 about the condition of the G.N.R's Royal Saloon, a new vehicle was subsequently designed by Patrick Stirling. It was built at the Plant during 1876 at a cost of £1474 and featured four-wheeled bogies; the Plant had commenced building bogie vehicles in 1875. The new saloon, No. 1691, was 38ft 6in. long, 8ft wide and weighed 22 tons. The interior consisted of two compartments with a servants' room at one end and a retiring room at the other. It was also fitted with leather upholstery instead of the usual cloth lining. A new Royal saloon, built in 1888 for the G.N.R. by Craven Bros of Sheffield, was unpopular with the Prince. As a result the 1876 saloon continued to be used by Royalty until later in the century. The interior and exterior of the vehicle are illustrated.

Stirling's 2-2-2 – Although the 8ft 'Singles' were Stirling's most noted locomotives, The Plant also produced, 36 smaller 'Singles' which had varying sizes of driving wheels. A group of 12 'Singles' was built between 1868-70 with 7ft 1in. driving wheels, a solitary locomotive appeared in 1870 with 7ft 7in. wheels and during 1885-1894 a batch of 23 engines was erected with 7ft 6in wheels. No. 232, belongs to the latter group and was built in 1885. Other Stirling locomotive characteristics are displayed here, include the domeless boiler, narrow rounded cab and the running plate carried straight and low from the buffer beam to the cab. Unfortunately the location of the photograph, taken around the turn of the century, is unknown but it might be near Doncaster Carr locomotive shed, where No. 232 was allocated for most of its life-span, being withdrawn in 1906.

Stirling's 2-4-0 – During the 1860s Stirling designed a 2-4-0 secondary main-line standard locomotive, intended for use on 'slow passenger', 'fast parcels' and 'goods' trains. Between 1867 and 1895, the year of Stirling's death, 139 of these locomotives were built, 114 at Doncaster. No. 755, illustrated, belongs to this group and was built c. 1896. Ivatt, who succeeded Stirling subsequently modified his predecessor's 2-4-0 locomotive to suit his own specifications, and a large number were rebuilt including No. 755 in 1906. The locomotive was fitted with a 'domed' boiler but retained a 'Stirling' cab, being finally withdrawn as No. 3755 in 1923.

Brass Finishers – Brass Finishers alongside Stirling 4-2-2 Single No. 93, built in 1879, displaying characteristic brass work used on Stirling locomotives including the graceful safety valve cover pictured in the centre of the photograph.

The Blacksmiths – Doncaster's character was completely altered by the coming of the railways. In the 1850s it was a quiet market town with a population of just under 6,000 people but by the turn of the century it had been transformed into a busy industrial centre with a population of 30,000. People from Lincolnshire, Nottinghamshire, East Anglia, the South East and the Midlands converged on Doncaster to find work with the town's new industry. They settled in scores of terraced houses built in Hyde Park and Hexthorpe which became known as the town's railway suburbs. A terrace in Hyde Park even bore a plaque 'Engine Men's Cottages.' A unique glimpse at the dress and general character of the people who worked at the Plant during the late 19th century is provided by this photograph. The men depicted are thought to be blacksmiths.

Patrick Stirling – Patrick Stirling (seated with cane) poses with Works Foremen outside the Turneries building including Works Manager John Shotton (two to the right of Stirling).

Stirling 0-6-0 Tender Engine – Locomotive No. 300 was completed in January 1889 and was one of 229 engines, mainly used on coal trains, erected between 1868 and 1895. Built as Works No. 479, the original 4' 2" diameter boiler was replaced in February 1911 by a larger 4'5" domed variety. The locomotive was finally withdrawn in August 1921.

Stirling's Singles – The first of Stirling's 4-2-2, 8ft 'Singles' was apparently built, in 1870, without any immediate need in mind. However, the locomotive, the most powerful at this time on the GNR, was quickly employed on express passenger trains. Between 1870-1895 a further 52 'Singles' were completed at the Plant. In an attempt to produce unprecedented cylinder horsepower from these locomotives and to lessen the risk of broken crank axles, a problem prevalent at this time, Stirling used 'outside' cylinders. He also introduced a four-wheel front bogie in preference to one with two wheels, since he considered that if 'outside' cylinders were used on the latter type of bogie the locomotive would sway from side to side and there would be excessive weight on the front axle. He therefore positioned the 'outside' cylinders between the two sets of wheels on the four-wheeled front bogies and in a horizontal line with the centre of the driving wheels. This introduced the engine's weight to the track progressively and avoided any unnecessary movement at high speed. Stirling's 'Single' No. 778, pictured here at the Plant, was built in 1887. By this time many of the 'Singles' in service had achieved impressive speed records earning them several pseudonyms including 'Highflyers'. A feature of the 'Singles' completed after 1881 was the plain 'splasher' accommodating an oval bras maker's plate, which can be seen in the illustration. No. 778 was withdrawn in 1904.

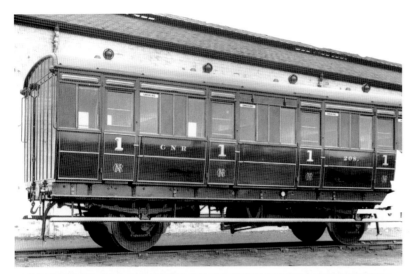

GNR Suburban First – This GNR Suburban First Class coach, No. 208 (Diagram 409) was built at The Plant in 1902. Comprising a total of 22 vehicles they had random numbering with an interior consisting of four separate First Class compartments. The vehicle was 28' 3" in length and and is shown here when new on 22 April 1902.

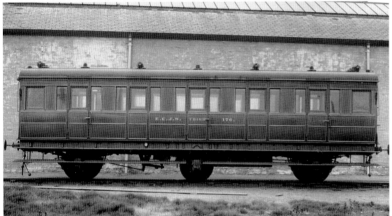

East Coast Joint Stock 6-wheeler– ECJS vehicle No 176 (Diagram 20) was built in 1891. The interior consisted of 30 seats, comprising end toilet, 5 3rd class compartments (with side corridor), and end toilet. The body length was 37' 2" and the vehicle was one of 16 built at Doncaster for the ECJS. Later it became GN Diagram 240 (in September 1922) but some were rebuilt to ECJS Diagram 5 (ECJS) on trains with first class coaches. The photograph was taken on outside the North Carriage Shed on 29 June 1916.

Stirling 0-4-4 Condensing Tank – No. 510 is a 120 Class 0-4-4 Back Tank built in 1874 and used on GNR London suburban services. The loco was one of 46 built, becoming GN Class G2. These locomotives were noticeable by their unique oval brass number plates instead of the customary yellow tracings. These were initially situated on the cab sides but in later years in the centre of the bunker side. This photograph from 1894 shows the locomotive as rebuilt with a large 4'5" diameter boiler in August 1892 but retaining its original 'built-up' chimney and early spring balance safety valves.

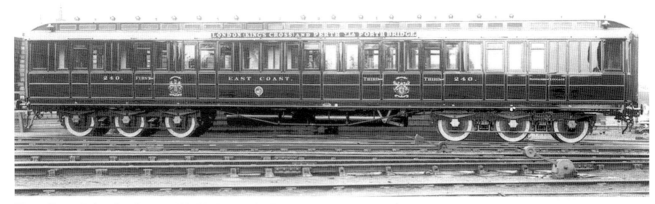

East Coast Joint Stock – In 1895/6 three train sets were built at The Plant to operate on East Coast Services. Each set consisted of 6 six-wheeled corridor bogie coaches and two six-wheeled Brake Vans. No. 240 pictured above c.1896 is an example of one of the six-wheeled bogie vehicles. This carriage was a First-Third Composite and its internal layout consisted of an end vestibule with toilet, First Class smoking compartment, First Class compartment, Third Class compartment, toilet, Third Class smoking compartment and a Guard's compartment. External features included bowed ends, centrally located gangway connections and clerestories with half domes at each end. In addition the corridor side of the vehicle had two 'dummy' doors.

ECJS Corridor Brake – Third No. 264 (ECJS Diagram 50) was one of 50 12-wheeled bogied vehicles, with no gangway ends, built at Doncaster during 1897. The vehicle is pictured as new outside the Works Carriage Shops.

Great Northern Express – A photograph taken at Bawtry, Doncaster in June 1900 of GNR Ivatt Atlantic 4-4-2 C1 class No. 984. The engine was built at Doncaster in June 1900 and the train here comprises coaches BTO 712, RFO 275, RKF 2838, RTO 2839, BTO (unidentified), and BG 1829.

The New Erecting Shop – This shop was built by the Doncaster firm of H Arnold & Son Ltd, on a site near the Forge and New Boiler Shop, in 1890-91, at a cost of £13,000. The new building consisted of two large erecting bays and a smaller bay for machinery. Both erecting bays accommodated a centre road with pits on either side. Each pit was capable of holding five engines. Two 30 ton overhead cranes, supplied by Messrs Craven Bros, Manchester, were housed in both of the erecting bays and were operated by cotton ropes, driven by a two cylinder steam wall engine. This view taken in October 1892 shows newly completed 0-4-4 Suburban Side Tank No 932 (centre) behind 0-4-2 mixed traffic tender locomotive No 32 undergoing repair. Partially out of sight to the left stands is 0-4-4 Suburban Back Tank No 624 receiving a larger 4'5" diameter boiler.

GNR Manchester Stock – GNR Manchester set pictured during 1898 in the Works Yard. The vehicles comprised (R to L) 799 BT, 2102 C, 1467 C, 486 C, 1421 BT. Diagrams 277 (Brake Third) and 129 (Composite). The Brake Third length 45' had an interior layout of: Guard, 3rd, Saloon 3rd, Toilet. The Composite vehicles (length 45') had an interior layout of: Lookout, 1st, Double Toilet, 1st, 3rd, Toilet.

GNR Corridor First – An external view of GNR Corridor 1st Dining Saloon No. 2836 which was built during the early part of 1899. It comprised:18 First Class seats and an interior layout comprising: Kitchen, Pantry (with toilet), Saloon 1st x 10, Toilet (with side corridor), Vestibule. These were three vehicles built as Nos 2836-8 and were normally run with an Open Third. The vehicle was rebuilt c.1914 with large windows (float glass) and subsequently reclassified to a Third Class Diner in 1929 and withdrawn ten years later. The photo was taken during March 1899.

1st Class Dining Saloon – Interior of 1st Class Dining Corridor Saloon No. 2836 (GN Diagram 52).

New Crimpsall Repair Shop – By the mid-1890s Ivatt discovered to his dismay that 'heavy' repairs to locomotives were being carried out at several running sheds, on the GNR network, instead of at the Plant. This was because the Plant's workshops were, at this time, unable to cope with the increasing GNR locomotive stock. As a result of consultation between Ivatt and the GNR Board it was decided to construct a new engine repair shop on the Crimpsall meadows adjacent to the Plant Works. The scheme began in 1899 after difficulties over the sale of the land were overcome. Construction work was carried out by local builders H. Arnold & Son Ltd at a cost of £294, 000. On completion, c.1901, the Crimpsall Locomotive Repair Shop had two small and four large bays. All the large bays had four repair pits and a 'stripping' pit in the centre road. The entire workshop could hold around 100 engines.

New Tender Shop – During 1900 tender repair work was moved to a new building (shown here under construction) at the west end of the Crimpsall Repair Shop. The New Tender Shop had two large repair bays with a smaller machine bay and could hold 32 tenders. In the early 1930s tender repairs were transferred to No.1 bay of the Crimpsall Engine Repair Shop. The New Tender Shop then became known as the Stripping Shop since its three bays were adapted for the stripping of locomotives, heavy boiler repairs and the repair of superheater flue and boiler tubes. During the 1960s the Stripping Shop was renamed the Locomotive Dismantling Shop. Diesel locomotives undergoing classified repairs were stripped here and the components crated, washed and examined before being dispatched to other repair sections.

Plant Fire Brigade – The Plant Fire Service was formed c.1880 and a resident Brigade established in 1908. Members of the Plant Brigade are pictured here in action.

New Paint Shop – The Locomotive Paint Shop is seen here under construction during April 1900. The building had eight roads with shallow pits and the roof was designed in a way to allow the north light to illuminate the interior. Paint storage was confined to the east end of the building, which also housed machinery used in grinding and mixing colour. The demand for compressed air in The Plant was met in the mid-1930s when a central compressor station was established in the Paint Shop. It consisted of three compressors of 750 cu. ft capacity directly coupled to 157 HP electric motors. The compressors were supplied by Messrs Fullerton, Hodgart and Barclay of Paisley. Under the 1987 Plant re-organisation scheme the Paint Shop became a storage area, locomotives being painted in the Crimpsall Repair Shop.

ECJS Dining Saloon – An interior view of an ECJS 3rd Dining Saloon nos 313-315. This was EJCS Diagram 30, built at Doncaster in 1900. After construction the vehicles were considered rather too opulent for Third Class passengers. Some vehicles were equipped with partitions between the seat backs to provide passenger privacy.

Composite Dining Car – A Composite Dining Car No. 2993 (GN Diagram 65) was built in 1901. It comprised: 18 First and 12 Third Class seats. The interior layout was Vestibule, Saloon 3rd x 12, Toilet Pantry Kitchen Pantry (all with side corridor), Saloon 1st x 4, Saloon 1st x 4, Twin Toilets and Vestibule. Four vehicles were built as Nos 2993-6 and later they were all rebuilt in some way. This vehicle (along with 2994) was rebuilt to Diagram 78A in c.1913 with large float glass glazing and an enlarged kitchen in place of the 1st x 4 Saloons.

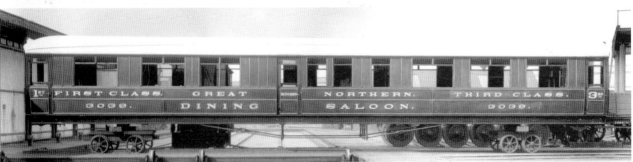

Composite Dining Car – Composite Dining Car No. 3039 (GN Diagram No 60) was built at Doncaster in 1906. It comprised 8 First Class and 18 Third Class seats, and an interior layout of Vestibule, Saloon, 8 x 1st, Pantry-Kitchen-Pantry (all with side corridor), Saloon 18 x 3rd, Vestibule. The body length was 65' 6" and Nos 3039 is shown in experimental livery as the first Gresley General Service Restaurant Car & first vehicle to carry elongated characters. The vehicle was transferred to NE Area in 1933 as 22262. The picture shows the body waiting fitting out on accommodation wheels on the Main Carriage Shop traverser during 1906.

GNR

Ivatt's First 'Atlantic' – By the 1890s it became clear that Stirling's 'Singles' were unable to cope with the increasing demand and changing character of express passenger work. In an attempt to alleviate the problem, Ivatt produced a locomotive with a 4-4-2 or 'Atlantic' wheel arrangement. His design had been inspired by similar engines built in 1895 by the Baldwin Locomotive Works in the USA for the Philadelphia & Reading Railroad. Ivatt was impressed with reports that these locomotives were achieving the fastest locomotive speeds in the world on their daily runs between Camden and Atlantic City. No 990 was built at Doncaster during 1898. It was an immense size when compared with other contemporary British locomotives and its characteristics were opposite to those of Stirling's engines. Ivatt favoured a large boiler with a large firebox, increasing the heating surface with cylinders of moderate dimensions. In contrast Stirling's main locomotive characteristics were small boiler and large cylinders. However, Stirling's 'Singles' had a greater tractive effort than the 'Atlantics' though this was counteracted by the latter's increased adhesion weight. Following the success of the first 'Atlantic' (later named Henry Oakley after a noted GNR General Manager), Doncaster built a further 21 locomotives of this type, between 1900 & 1903.

The Plant's Crane Engine – This locomotive was originally built at Doncaster during 1876 as an 0-4-4, Stirling designed, back tank, No. 553. Following withdrawal 29 years later the locomotive underwent a variety of alterations and survived for a number of years as a Doncaster Works' crane, used for material handling and carriage brake testing. Despite its utilitarian role it was painted in fully lined-out GNR green livery. The locomotive was finally condemned on 23rd November 1928, the only Stirling 0-4-4 Tank to last until LNER days.

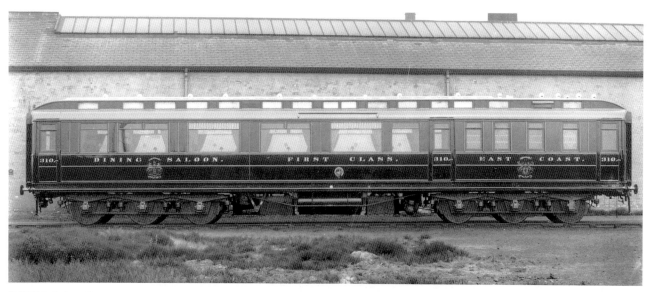

ECJS Dining Saloon – An ECJS First Dining Saloon No. 310 (ECJS Diagram 76A). It was built to Diagram 76 in 1900 and rebuilt with large 'float glass' windows (as seen here) in July 1913. It included 20 seats , Interior Vestibule, Saloon, Saloon, Kitchen (with corridor). Three were built as Nos. 310-312. This vehicle was transferred to GNR stock at 1929 as 43246 to GN Diagram 53.

Howlden's Last Vehicles – First Class Dining Car No. 2581, built at the Plant in 1904, was probably one of Carriage Superintendent F Howlden's last designs before he retired during the following year. Many features of carriage design and development which were introduced during Howlden's term of office, are represented in this vehicle. They include six-wheeled bogies, electric lighting, clerestory roofs (with bowed ends) vacuum brakes, corridors, vestibules and gangway connections. No 2531 was 62ft long and weighed 40 tons 8 cwt. The internal layout comprised a vestibule, toilet, smoking saloon with eight seats, non smoking saloon with ten seats, vestibule, pantry, kitchen and vestibule. Part of one of the saloons is shown here.

Class C1 Large Atlantic – In 1902 there emerged from The Plant a much more impressive and enormous 'Atlantic' than 'Henry Oakley'. The new locomotive had a much larger boiler, grate area, and heating surface. Following the customary, routine test period, a further 93 locomotives were built between 1902-1910, 92 at Doncaster and the remaining one, a four cylinder compound, at Vulcan Foundry. The boiler and frames of the first Class C1 4-4-2 Large Atlantic No. 251 can be seen in the New Erecting Shop during the early part of 1901.

Pictured in the middle photograph is Ivatt's penultimate Large Atlantic No 1460 with its traincrew. Completed in November 1910 with a Schmidt 18-element superheater and piston valves as standard, the locomotive would further benefit from a Robinson 24-element superheater (May 1917) and 31-element type (June 1931) before final withdrawal from service in October 1945.

Ivatt's 'Large Atlantic' – No. 1415, picture on the turntable near Doncaster station on 27 April 1923, was completed during 1908. When these 'large Atlantics', as they became known, entered service, they were more powerful than anything hitherto seen hauling British express passenger trains. Later, Gresley, who succeeded Ivatt in 1911, made refinements and adjustments to the Class and despite two locomotives being withdrawn in 1924 and 1927 most existed until after the Second World War. Several locomotives after withdrawal were used as stationary boilers and could be seen in Doncaster at The Plant and the Wagon Works.

GNR First Saloon – The interior of GNR First Saloon No. 3099 built in 1908 (Diagram 4). Photographed when new on 10 September. This vehicle was later included in the ECJS Royal Train.

GNR First Dining Car – An interior view of the main dining saloon, from the vestibule end, of First Class 'Harrogate' Dining Car No 3250. Note the wallpaper and fine ceiling detail. The vehicle was built in October 1912 to Diagram 76.

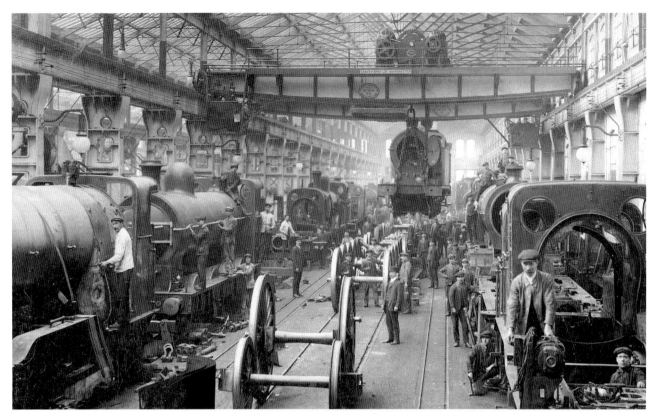

The Crimpsall Interior – The Crimpsall Repair Shop, when working to capacity could repair 100 engines and 16 tenders. The average time taken to carry out heavy repairs to a locomotive was about 60 working days. Workers operated in groups or gangs, under the supervision of a charge-hand, and had six or seven engines in the course of dismantling or re-erecting at any one time. An engine received in the Crimpsall Repair Shop for repairs was partially stripped on the centre road of a bay, lifted off its wheels and placed on an erecting pit where stripping was completed. The various parts were transported, via trolley roads and electric tractors, to the boiling and cleaning tanks, and subsequently distributed to the various shops for repairs or replacement. The re-erection of the engine commenced when the repairable parts were dealt with and parts for replacement manufactured. This photograph first appeared in the May 1913 edition of the Railway Magazine.

The Crimpsall Repair Shop consisted of four large bays (1-4) 520 ft long by 52 ft wide and two smaller bays (1A and 3A) each 30ft wide for machine fitters, coppersmiths and boilersmiths. This picture also appeared in the May 1913 edition of the Railway Magazine.

ECJS Royal Saloon – A photograph dating from 4 April 1908 of the ECJS Royal Saloon No. 395 under construction in the Main Carriage Shop at Doncaster Works. It was built by the GNR at Doncaster for HM King Edward VII. The body length was 67' 0" to ECJS Diagram 81. Later the vehicle was refurbished for Queen Mary and the Queen Mother. The accommodation as built included Vestibule, Toilet, Dressing Room, Bedroom, Saloon, Smoking Room, Toilet. In subsequent years it was converted to: Vestibule, Toilet, Toilet, Dressing Room, Private Saloon, Day Saloon, Saloon, Vestibule. In later years the saloon was also used by Queen Elizabeth II, and now resides at the National Railway Museum at York.

King Edward's Dressing Room – This photograph taken on 11 September 1908 shows the elegant interior of King Edward's VII's Dressing Room.

The GNR Royal Train – with ECJS Royal Saloon No. 395 (fourth carriage from the front) taken in the Plant Works yard on 10 September 1908.

GNR

The Carr Wagon Works – Wagon construction and repair was carried out at the Plant until 1889, when the work was transferred to a site at the Carr, two miles south of the town. The move was initiated by the need for more space within the Plant and to ease congestion around the main-line station area, caused by wagons waiting to be repaired or despatched. Congestion problems were lessened at the Carr since the new buildings were in close proximity to marshalling yards, where wagons could be conveniently manoeuvred and stored. Workmen from Doncaster were taken to and from the Carr everyday by a special train. There were two main buildings at the Carr, the North Shop and the South Shop. New Wagon construction took place in the North shop which had seven working roads capable of holding around 140 wagons. It also contained a steam hammer, woodworking machinery, drilling machines, wheel and axle lathes and a boring machine for wagon bearings. The South Shop was used for repair work and had 15 roads, 10 of which were used as working roads. The entire shop could hold around 220 wagons. The GNR's drays, vans and road vehicles were also built there. A small building nearby was used as the Wagon Paint Shop. Many different types of wagons were built at the Carr including Open Wagons, Goods Brakes, Horse Boxes, Gas Tanks, Fish Vans and Breakdown Cranes. Construction work continued until re-grouping in 1923 when the Wagon shops' main function was to repair and recondition all types of stock. Wagon work at the Carr lasted until 1964/5 when the Wagon Shops were transferred back to the main Plant complex. This view, taken on 8th May 1908, from Red Bank Bridge, shows the North Shop.

Carr Wagon Works – Painting and stencilliing in c1916

GNR

Carr Wagon Works – Painting of GNR 7-plank wagons (left) and ventilated vans in 1916.

Plant Panorama – Although the photograph below was taken, c.1912 from the top of Doncaster's St George's Church, to illustrate the new North Bridge, it also gives a unique view of part of the Plant Works. From left to right, beyond the bridge, the Plant buildings are the West Carriage Shop, Grease Shop, Tank House and North Carriage Shed. A splendid array of vintage GNR rolling stock is also visible together with several locomotives, including a Stirling 0-4-2 and an Ivatt 'Atlantic.' During the early 1960s the West carriage Shop and North Carriage Shed were adapted for the maintenance of the DMUs.

Iron Foundry – The Works Iron Foundry was constructed during 1881. Comprising a large centre bay and two small side bays. Separating the bays were two rows of cast iron columns which also supported the roof structure and housed the rails for an overhead crane. Originally the crane was operated from the shop floor by rope. Initially, there was only one cupola for melting iron and the 'blast' was produced by a steam driven 'Roots' blower. During the late 1880s the Foundry's equipment was modernised; a sand riddling machine was introduced in 1887 and two 'Darling and Sellars' moulding machines were purchased in 1889. Three years later the manoeuvre of metal ladles became easier by the installation of a 15 ton overhead, steam-driven crane (illustrated here) obtained from J. Booth & Bros of Rodley, Leeds. During the present century the Iron Foundry has played an important role in manufacturing many of the parts of the famous Plant-built steam locomotives. Following the demise of steam traction h owever, during the mid-1960s, the Iron Foundry became redundant and was converted for use as a Crane and Chain Repair Shop.

GNR

GNR class H2 – Work taking place in the New Erecting shop on 5 December 1912 on GNR class H2 (K1) Mogul 2-6-0 No. 1633.

No. 1633 – No. 1633 is pictured ready for painting on 29 March 1913.

Gresley's K1 – Following Gresley's appointment as GNR Locomotive Superintendent he realised that the Company was short of 'express goods' engines. To meet this need he produced, in 1912, a 2-6-0 locomotive, G.R Class H2 No 1630. Besides the unusual 2-6-0 wheel arrangement the locomotive featured Walschaerts valve gear and a running plate above the wheels, both of which were not familiar on GNR locomotives. A further nine engines were completed at Doncaster in 1913 and all the Class were quickly employed on 'express goods', 'mixed traffic' and during the First World war, on a number of 'hospital' trains. Crews, however, often complained the locomotives gave an uneasy ride and afforded them the title 'ragtimers' after a lively contemporary dance of the same title. In 1914 after analysing the locomotives under traffic conditions, Gresley realised the 20in. diameter cylinders were too large for the boiler capacity. He subsequently produced 75 locomotives with a Robinson 24 element superheater in place of the Schmidt type previously employed. Furthermore the shape of the cab windows, instead of being round, as on the earlier 2-6-0s, followed the contour of the cab and fire-box sides. At Grouping in 1923 the first ten 2-6-0s became Class K1 and the later batch Class K2. In later years the K1s were re-boilered and became reclassified as K2's.

Carriage Repairs – In 1890/1 a major expansion of the Works saw the construction of the West Carriage Shop and North Carriage Shed for the repair of GNR and ECJS coaches. Pictured in c1916 Coach Repairers undertake a variety of bench work repairs in the West Carriage Shop on bogied and 6-wheeled rolling stock.

Coach Repairers – A line up of Coach Repairers many pictured on the photograph above in front of coach No. 3074 c1916.

West Carriage Shop – A view in the West Carriage Shop on 20 March 1913 showing a Wheel Pinch in use for manoeuvring and turning wheels by 'walking' them around in the manner shown. This method was superseded by the introduction of Simpson's Patent wheel swivel design to lift and support the axle about its centre.

Carriage Repairs – Repairs taking place on vehicle No. 3047 and the other GNR carriages in 1916. Notice the degree of bowing in the wooden underframes of the longer bogied carriages on the left.

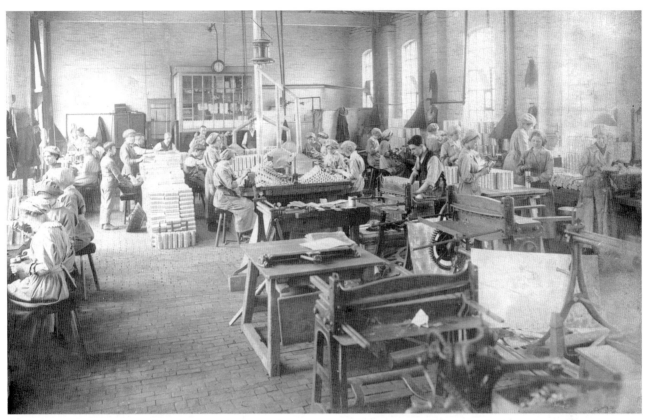

War Work at the Plant – Following the outbreak of hostilities in 1914 the Plant prepared for the introduction of War work. In September 1914, 750 ambulance stretchers were produced in the Carriage shops. A month later there was a meeting between Sir Frederick Donaldson of the Woolwich Arsenal and several leading railway company engineers to decide how their workshops could provide help for the war effort. As a result Doncaster Works, in collaboration with the North-Eastern Railway Company, agreed to manufacture parts for 150 eighteen-pounder field guns. The work required extreme accuracy and was skilfully carried out by the Plant employees. From 1915, six inch shells and gun mountings were manufactured and work was also carried out on reconditioning and repairing eighteen-pounder cartridge cases. Initially trade apprentices worked on the cartridge cases but as the War became prolonged they were replaced by women, who became employed on a variety of tasks within the Plant. The picture shows women involved in the manufacture of tin fuse cylinders.

Women War workers in the Drilling Section at the Carr Wagon Shops c.1916.

Reforming Cartridge Cases – Following several interviews between Lloyd George (Minister for Munitions) and Nigel Gresley, the Plant began producing six-inch, high explosive shells weighing 100lbs each. Most of the tasks involved in this type of work were carried out by women, who operated day and night shifts on Sundays as well as week days. Complete shells were not produced at the Plant but were made ready to be sent on to the 'filling' factory. Other important war work included the 'reforming' of 18 lb cartridge cases seen here on 24th June 1916 in the old Boiler (Now No1 bay, D shop).

Cartridge Cases – Cartridge cases pictured outside D1 Shop during July 1915.

Gresley's 'Ardsley' Tank – Around 1913 Gresley set himself the task of designing a new tank engine. The result was the 0-6-0, J51 locomotive. With this engine he abandoned the use of saddle tanks which had been favoured by the GNR since Sturrock's day in favour of side tanks. These extended along the boiler and smoke box and were sloped at the forward end to improve visibility and cut away beneath to access the locomotive's motion. The locomotive also had greater brake power and adhesion than the earlier engines. The initial engines were allocated to Ardsley depot, Leeds gaining the nickname 'Ardsley Tanks'. A further 30 were built at the plant between 1914-1919. Later the design was modified and a further 72 locomotives were produced (58 at Doncaster) from 1922-1939. These engines were classified J50.

Eden Grove – Picture taken on the opening of Eden Grove sports Ground in 1914, situated to the west of the Crimpsall shops which catered for The Plant's sports needs. On the left on the back row is the young Nigel Gresley.

King's Cross-Leeds Quintuple Set – A quintuple set of articulated coaches was produced at the Plant in 1921, especially for the King's Cross-Leeds express service which left the capital at 10.10 am and started the return journey at 5.30 pm. The set comprised a Brake First, First Diner, Kitchen Car, Third Diner and Brake Third. Before entering passenger service extensive tests were carried out to determine if the stock was sufficiently stable at high speed. One test involved filling tumblers to the brim with water and placing them on the tables of the Dining Cars. Even at speeds exceeding 60 mph very little spillage occurred. The Kitchen Car contained, for the first time in Britain, electric cooking equipment. Whilst the train was in motion, dynamos driven from the Kitchen Car's bogie axles, charged the batteries used by the cooking equipment. However, during the time the Kitchen Car spent in the two terminal stations, electricity was obtained via leads plugged into ground mains to avoid the batteries being drained of power. As all the vehicles were expected to operate exclusively on the King's Cross-Leeds service 'destinations' were painted on the carriage roofs, instead of the more conventional, removable boards. The quintuple set is seen here on 23rd September 1921.

Gresley's K3 – Gresley re-designed his 2-6-0 mixed traffic locomotive during 1920 and produced a engine, No. 1000, which had three cylinders, a 6ft diameter boiler and twin regulator handles. In place of the rocking shaft previously employed on the three cylinder 2-8-0 locomotive, to work the inside valve, a simplified conjugated gear, in the form of rocking levers in the ratio 2:1 was used. The 6ft boiler caused a sensation in the railway world, since it was the first time that a British locomotive had been fitted with a boiler of this size. The two regulator handles, one on either side of the firebox, which later became a standard feature on steam locomotives, enabled the driver to work on both sides of the cab when manoeuvring in busy marshalling yards. Between 1920-1937 a further 192 locomotives were built (30 of these at Doncaster) becoming LNER Class K3. The locomotives were largely employed on 'express goods' and 'fish' trains. No 1001 is pictured here on 3nd June 1920 shortly after completion.

Gresley's First 'Pacific' – By the early 1920s an express passenger locomotive with greater power than the 'Atlantic' was needed. In an attempt to find a solution to this problem Gresley re-appraised the designs he had made in 1915 for a 'Pacific' or 4-6-2 engine in the light of the success of his three cylinder 2-6-0 and 2-8-0 locomotives. He also studied the information published on the renowned, well proportioned, Pennsylvanian Railroad K4 'Pacific' of 1911. As a result Gresley designed a handsome three cylinder 4-6-2 locomotive, which was built during 1922 at Doncaster. The engine was numbered 1470 and named 'Great Northern' before it left The Plant. The locomotive is pictured being lifted in the New Erecting Shop on 24th March 1922 (centre) and later on 23rd May following completion.

The Prince of Wales at the Plant – The future King Edward VIII in November 1926 accompanied by Nigel Gresley and the Mayor of Doncaster. Stirling Single No1 and Gresley's P1 2-8-2 'Mikado' No 2394 stand in the background.

Carriage Trimming Shop – Workers pictured in the Carriage Trimming Shop during May 1930. This Shop was built in 1866 as an extension beyond the station footbridge to the north of the Turneries Buildings (now Denison House). During the Second World War the Chief Mechanical Engineer's Office was relocated from King's Cross back to The Plant and housed in this building.

GNR Football Saloon interior – Built in 1908 at Doncaster to GN Diagram 21, GNR Football Saloon No 1377N shows the relatively sparse internal decoration of these vehicles. Taken on 7 December 192, the vehicle has just passed into LNER ownership.

Sheffield Rotarians Visit – Sheffield Rotary Club paid a visit to the Works on 15 May 1928 and members are seen here along with Works Manager Robert A.Thom (eighth from the left) in front of Class A1 Pacific No. 4474 Victor Wild (the fifth Gresley Pacific and two after Flying Scotsman).

LNER

LNER

Institution of Locomotive Engineers – Members of the Institution of Locomotive Engineers are seen here on a visit to the Works on 14 June 1927. They have been photographed in front of an unidentified Class A1 Pacific. Nigel Gresley may be seen at the front of the photograph with Robert Thom to the right.

LNER

'Flying Scotsman' – The third A1 to be completed was No. 4472 'Flying Scotsman'. It emerged from the Plant during February 1923 and no one at this time could have foreseen that it was destined to become one of the most famous steam locomotives in the world. In 1924 Flying Scotsman along with Stockton & Darlington Railway No1 'Locomotion' of 1825 were displayed on the LNER stand in the Palace of Engineering at the British Empire Exhibition at Wembley where the locomotive is seen being delivered.

A1s and A3s – By the mid-1920s 52 A1 locomotives had been built (32 at Doncaster). Although the locomotives coped with East Coast passenger trains adequately, their coal consumption was rather high. Gresley found the answer to this problem in 1925, when the LNER and GWR exchanged express passenger locomotives for test trials. On the LNER routes, the GWR locomotive 'Pendennis Castle' proved to have a lower fuel consumption because it had 'long lap' valves. Consequently, these type of valves were fitted on all the A1s. Two years later in a further effort to improve the A1s performance, it was decided to use 19 in. diameter cylinders and to increase the working boiler pressure from 180 lb./sq. in. to 220 lb/sq. in., incorporating a 43 element superheater. All the new 'Pacific' locomotives built after 1928 incorporated these new features and became classified as A3s. Gresley also decided that all existing A1s should be rebuilt as A3s, when new boilers were required. In March 1935 No 2750 'Papyrus' was used by Gresley to determine whether a high-speed service could be run eventually between London and the North East. Hauling a 213 ton train 'the locomotive' achieved a record 108 mph and laid the foundation for the introduction of the 'Silver Jubilee' service in september 1935. 'Papyrus' is seen here following its record-breaking run.

'Cock O' the North' – During the early 1930s, Gresley began designing a locomotive that could handle the formidable work between Edinburgh and Aberdeen, where train loads reached 550 tons or more and routes presented severe gradients and sharp curves. The new locomotive when it appeared from the Plant in May 1934, was the largest and most powerful engine that had ever been built in Britain. Class P2, No 2001 'Cock O' the North' had an overall length of 73ft 8 ¾ in and a 'Mikado' 2-8-2 wheel arrangement. The eight-coupled wheels provided the required adhesion and tractive effort for the Scottish terrain. Another P2 Earl Marischal appeared from the Plant in 1934 and four more in 1936. All were given names which had some historical association with the area where they were intended to operate. 'Cock O' the North was a pseudonym given to George, the fifth Duke of Gordon.

'Cock O' the North' – In this photograph of 12th May 1934 can be seen (left to right) R A Thom, Mechanical Engineer, E Windle, Chief Locomotive Draughtsman, J S Jones, Assistant Works Manager, J Eggleshaw, Works Manager, two chargehand fitters and the foreman of the New Erecting Shop and on the far right the Paint Shop Foreman. Behind the group can be seen the ACFI boiler feed water heater (later removed). After running trials over the summer of 1934 the locomotive was shipped to France in November, accompanied by Gresley's assistant Oliver Bulleid for testing on the French locomotive test plant at Vitry. Whilst abroad the locomotive ran several main line test runs between Orleans and Tours.

Gresley's V1 – A new type of LNER 2-6-2 tank engine, emerged from the Plant in 1930. The Class V1 was largely intended for use on suburban duties and a total of 82 were Plant-built between 1930-1939. The latter year saw the introduction of 10 V3 Class engines which were essentially a modified version of the V1 with a higher boiler pressure. The Plant was also responsible in subsequent years for the conversion of most of the V1 engines to V3. V1 No 2909 is seen newly outshopped on 3rd October 1931. The locomotive was converted to Class V3 by October 1953 and was withdrawn during February 1962.

Gresley's Streamlined Pacifics – By the early 1930s high speed, diesel-electric passenger trains were being operated in America and Germany. Consequently the LNER Board instructed Gresley to approach the builders of the German diesel rail cars with an order for a three coach diesel-electric unit, which would operate a four hour schedule between Newcastle and King's Cross. However, the Germans could not meet the LNER's requirements since their unit was incapable of beating a time of four and a half hours and the passenger accommodation was unsatisfactory. Gresley was subsequently asked if the Class A1 or A3 locomotives could be adapted to meet the Company's specifications. As a result of carrying out various tests with one of the Class A3 locomotives and experiments with several 'front-end' shapes, to determine which gave least resistance to head winds, he produced a new engine. This was 'Pacific' Class A4 No. 2509 'Silver Link' which was completed at the Plant in September 1935.

Besides meeting the LNER's needs, the locomotive had a striking appearance with its Bugatti-type 'wedge' nose and tri-colour silver-grey paint work. One writer on railway history even described it as an apparition. Although the A3 'Pacific' design had been utilised as the basis of the A4, the latter had higher boiler pressure, larger piston valves and a lower fuel consumption, partly attributed to the streamlined body No. 2509 immediately entered service on the Newcastle-King's Cross 'Silver Jubilee' train, which was named in honour of the Silver Jubilee of George V and Queen Mary. All the A4 Class, consisting of 35 locomotives, were Plant-built. No. 4499 is seen here. All 35 Class A4 locomotives were built at the Plant. No 4499 'Pochard' was completed in April 1938 two months after 'Mallard'.

Class A3 Pacific – Class A3 Pacific No. 2598 Blenheim is seen on 12 September 1936 in the New Erecting Shop undergoing centre of gravity experiments with an empty boiler. Scribed lines on the lifting plate show the difference between an empty and full boiler.

'P2s' streamlined – During 1936 when the remaining four of the P2 Class (Nos 2003-2006) were under construction, it was decided that the front of the locomotives should be fitted with a streamlined casing as on the A4 Class. However, the casing finished behind the smokebox and an 'ordinary' boiler was retained. Furthermore side valances were not fitted to the P2s. The first two Class P2 locomotives built in 1934 were also streamlined in 1937 (No 2002) and 1938 (No 2001). The third Class P2 locomotive No. 2003 Lord President is pictured in the Crimpsall on 3 April 1938 probably on its first major overhaul from new. With their long wheelbase the P2's were prone to wear in the side rods and had the flanges of the two centre wheels narrowed to aid passage around curved track.

LNER

Silver Jubilee Train – Taken inside the First Class Restaurant Car on the inaugural run of the 'Silver Jubilee' on 30th September 1935 after arrival at King's Cross. The photographer's journalist colleague is completing his report for telephoning back to the North East. Despite the radical external streamline appearance of the train, the interior was of more conventional styling.

Silver Jubilee train headed by A4 4-6-2 No. 2509 Silver Link at Barkstown North Junction on a trial run in October 1935. Construction of the seven coach Silver Jubilee train was authorised in February 1935 and constructed in the Works Main Carriage Shop. The train comprised two articulated twins and a restaurant/kitchen car triplet.

'Green Arrow' Express Freight – The LNER introduced a special registered goods service in 1936 known as the 'Green Arrow' Service. Designs for a new locomotive to be used on this service had begun a year earlier. The new engine Class V2 No. 4771 was named 'Green Arrow'. A mixed traffic 2-6-2 locomotive, it had 6ft 2in diameter coupled wheels and was followed by four more Nos 4772-4775. The V2 was similar in appearance to the A3 'Pacifics' but its boiler had a shorter barrel. Steam collection was through a banjo-shaped dome, although a completely new front end was designed with three cylinders, steam chests and smokebox-saddle, all being part of one monobloc casting. Walschaerts valve gear was fitted to the 'outside' cylinders and the Gresley-derived motion was applied to the 'inside' cylinder valve. Standard 4200 gallon tenders were fitted and by the time the building ceased in 1944 (when Thompson stopped the last four locomotives being constructed) there were 184 engines in this Class. Only eight locomotives were named. Apart from 'Green Arrow', there were two named after public schools and five after famous regiments. From their introduction the V2s proved themselves on 'fast goods' trains. In World War II they hauled trains of up to 26 carriages, weighing approximately 850 tons.

'Coronation Train' – The commercial success and popularity with the general public of the 'Silver Jubilee' trains led to further streamlined sets being produced at the Plant. Both the 'Coronation' and 'West Riding Ltd' sets were built in 1937. The 'Coronation' was named in honour of King George VI's coronation and operated between London and Edinburgh. Here Observation Cars for the Coronation train are under construction in the Main Carriage Shop on 10th May 1937.

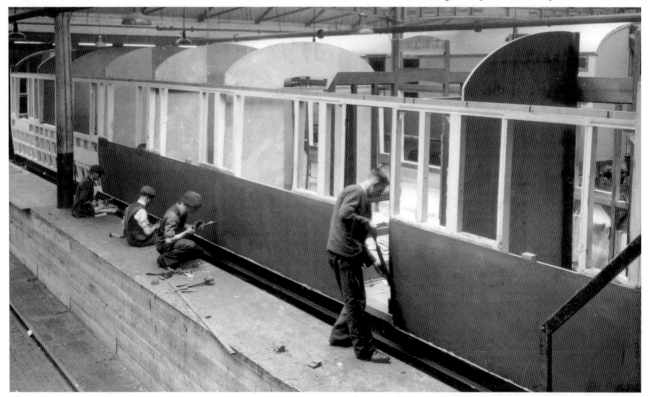

Each 'Coronation' train consisted of four twin articulated coaches: a Brake Third, Open Third, Kitchen Third, Open Third, two Open Firsts, Kitchen Third and Brake Third. Although there were two Kitchen Cars in each train set, there were no Restaurant Cars as it was intended that all passengers should be served with meals at their 'normal' seats. All the vehicles (with seating) had centre gangways but as open stock was not popular, the First and Third Class saloons were divided by partitions. The coaches were teak framed with steel body panels and the exterior was painted in Marlborough and Garter Blue. The roofs were spray-painted in aluminium finish, the bogies were painted black and the wheels were red. Messrs Acton Surgery Ltd were responsible for the design of the internal decor and there was a strong use of rexine together with anodised aluminium fret trims. Here Coronation Kitchen Third to diagram 230/228 is having steel skinning applied in the Main Carriage shop on 10th May 1937.

During the summer a beaver-tailed Observation Car was attached to the rear of the Coronation Train. It accommodated 16 passengers who paid one shilling (5p) to occupy a swivel armchair for an hour. These vehicles also provided a matching 'Bugatti' shape to the streamlined A4 'Pacific' at the front of the train.

The upholstery in the Third Class saloons was of uncut fawn moquette with green carpets. Wall coverings were in two shades of grey-green rexine and were divided by the fretted trim. Lavishly upholstered swivel armchairs, one on either side of the gangway, were fitted in the First Class saloons. The overall colour scheme was green. Pictured here is the Coronation Train Cinema Coach.

'Tommy' – During the 1930s the LNER produced ambitious plans for the electrification of the main-line between Manchester-Sheffield-Wath, using the 1500v D.C. overhead system. Unfortunately, the Second World War interrupted the scheme but the design and construction of a prototype 0-4-4-0 (Bo-Bo) mixed-traffic electric locomotive continued. No. 6701, pictured here, was designed by Nigel Gresley and completed at the Plant in 1940. It was tested on the Manchester South Junction and Altrincham Railway in 1941 but was put in storage for the rest of the War. The locomotive, renumbered by Thompson in 1946 to become No. 6000, was still idle after the War. The LNER however, was anxious for the locomotive to undergo more extensive trials before continuing production of further engines. Fortunately in September 1947, the Netherlands Railway agreed to run the locomotive for test trials. The Dutch nick-named the locomotive 'Tommy' (their name for a British soldier during the Second World War). When the locomotive returned to Britain in March 1952 it was given BR No. 26000 and bore a brass nameplate with the official name 'Tommy' on its side. Between 1950-1953 a further 57 locomotives were built, not at Doncaster but at Gorton. The 'Tommies' were used on the electrified route between Manchester-Sheffield-Wath, which opened in 1954 as the most modern railway line in Britain. Tommy was finally withdrawn in May 1970.

Top Photo – The locomotive under construction during 'blackout' conditions in the New Erecting Shop on 30th October 1939.

Middle Photo – Taken 6th April 1940 showing part fitted out body.

Bottom Photo – As new in green livery 4th February 1941.

Main Carriage Shop Fire – Carriage construction was curtailed at the Plant following an accidental fire on 21st December 1940. It completely destroyed the Main Carriage Building Shop and also caused an estimated £18, 000 worth of damage to existing coaching stock including the loss of a GN Dynamometer Car. The fire alerted enemy aircraft in the area and bombs were dropped in the Plant Yard, but fortunately, they did not explode. A replacement building was completed in 1949 and housed Fabrication, Assembly, Trimming, Upholstery and Joinery Shops and a Saw Mill. This photograph taken from the Drawing Office roof, shows the devastation caused by the fire.

American Service Personnel – American Service Personnel on parade at The Plant c. 1943

American GIs – American GIs celebrate Christmas 1943 with Plant staff on the cleared site of the Main Carriage Shop.

Bruce Woodcock – Bruce Woodcock, a former heavyweight boxing champion of Great Britain and the British Empire, worked for a time as a boiler fitter at the Plant during the Second World War. He is pictured here on locomotive No. 2459 on 1 August 1945.

Smiths Shop – During the war, much female labour was again employed on both war work and on conventional railway tasks. Here in 1942 a young lady operates a drop hammer in the Works' Smith Shop.

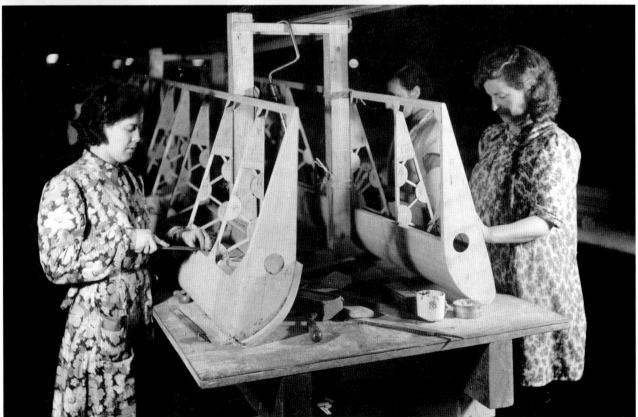

War Time Diversification – The Plant was again involved in war work during 1939-45. The type of work undertaken was as varied as it had been in the First World War and included the production of tank gun-plates, gun base-plates and anti-tank gun carriages. The Plant also gave assistance to other contractors carrying out war work. Here female workers assemble wooden glider wing sections.

LNER

The Plant's First Diesel Shunter – The financial burden of shunting operations was causing some concern for the main-line railway companies during the early 1930s. One of the suggestions submitted to reduce costs was to provide a substantial shunting locomotive which could be operated by one person. However, before this could be achieved a different type of motive power needed to be adopted and various experiments were carried out with diesel-mechanical, hydraulic and electric engines. Consequently, the LNER produced four, twin-motor, diesel-electric shunters, similar in design to an LMS version, at the Plant during 1944, Nos 8000-8003 (later BR Nos 15000-15003). These were the first diesel-electric locomotives built at Doncaster and more shunters were produced in the 1950s and 60s including a number of Class 03 and 08 locomotives.

Wartime intruders – Throughout the Second World War, LMS Stanier designed class 8F, 2-8-0 locomotives were built in considerable numbers for the Ministry of War Transport Division by private contractors as well as the four main-line railway companies. The LNER similar to the GWR and SR, were reluctant to build locomotives to another company's design but agreed to do so on the understanding that the locomotives could, after the cessation of hostilities, be transferred to the LMS. Between May 1943 and September 1945 the Plant built 30 of these engines, numbered 8510-8539. They were also lettered LMS since they were regarded as being on loan to the LNER. During 1943 the LNER agreed to build, in the interest of the nation and out of their own funds, a further batch of 68, 2-8-0s. Between October 1945 and June 1946, the Plant constructed 20 of these numbered 3148-3167 and lettered LNER. Later however, all the Stanier 2-8-0s built by the LNER workshops were transferred to the LMS. First Class 8F No.8510 is pictured at Doncaster Works on 27 May 1943.

Between 1942-44 almost 800 USA Class 160, 2-8-0 locomotives were shipped to the united Kingdom in preparation for the Allied invasion of Europe. They were originally intended for use by the US Army Transportation Corps personnel but the first 400 to reach Britain were employed by either the four main-line railway companies or the War Department. The Plant was amongst a number of railway workshops that adapted and modified these locomotives before they entered service in the United Kingdom. USA locomotive No. 1619 was pictured at Doncaster during 1943, shortly before it was transferred to the GWR.

East Anglian – An interior view of LNER Smoking Open First, built at Doncaster during 1937 to Diagram 237 for the East Anglian service. The photograph was taken on 21 April 1944 and shows typical interior styling of the 1930's.

Armoured Barbette Van – An RAF Armoured Barbette Van pictured on 2 October 1940. The vehicle was based on a Fordson Van, modified and fitted with armour plating at The Plant for use at RAF Hatfield.

Supreme Headquarters
ALLIED EXPEDITIONARY FORCE
Office of the Supreme Commander

15 April, 1945.

Dear Sir Ronald.

I must write to thank you personally, as Chairman of The London and North Eastern Railway, and all those members of your staff who have done such fine work on the new "Bayonet". I am indeed grateful to you.

Would you please extend my special thanks to Mr. E. Thompson and Mr. A. H. Peppercorn, the Chief and Assistant Chief Mechanical Engineers at Doncaster, who rendered such invaluable assistance to Colonel Bingham.

The wholehearted cooperation of the British Railways at all times during this war will always stand out as one of the finest examples of Anglo-Americanism.

With renewed thanks.

Sincerely
Dwight D. Eisenhower

Sir Ronald W. Matthews
Lime Tree Cottage
Letwell
Nr. Worksop
Notts., England

Eisenhower's 'Bayonet' Coach – Edward Thompson, Colonel Bingham (US Army) and Arthur Peppercorn after inspecting General Eisenhower's special armour-plated coach (codename 'Bayonet') on Monday 12 March 1945. This vehicle No. 1591, originally built in 1936 to Diagram 157 as a First Class Sleeping Car with ten single compartments was converted at Doncaster for war use.

Royal Visit – King George VI and Queen Elizabeth are shown on 29th October 1941 whilst inspecting the 46th WR (Don Thompson to the left. The photograph is taken between the former Turneries Building and D Shop (D5 bay).

Final Parade – In the early days of the Second World War a large group of Doncaster railwaymen formed a Home Guard. detachment, which numbered over 500 men, was to maintain the security of the Locomotive, Carriage and Wagon Works a Home guard is seen here on 3rd December 1944 during their final parade on the site of the former Main carriage Shop.

on Home Guard. Accompanying the Royal Party is Arthur Peppercorn looking anxiously toward the camera with Edward

as the LNER detachment and formed part of the local battalion, the 46th WR (Doncaster) Bn. Home guard. The role of the railway station and bridges. The men also took part in the Battalion's overall scheme for the town's protection. The LNER

LNER

Cock O' the North Rebuilt – Following the death of Sir Nigel Gresley in April 1941, Edward Thompson became LNER Chief Mechanical Engineer. It was a known fact that Gresley and Thompson detested each other. Consequently, the latter took the unpopular decision of rebuilding some of Gresley's locomotives under the guise of providing prototypes for new Classes. The engines that 'suffered' most under Thompson's regime were the 2-8-2 P2 Class which Gresley had designed for working over the formidable Scottish terrain. During January 1943 P2 No. 2005 'Thane of Fife' was rebuilt as a 'Pacific' locomotive. The Bugatti-type wedge-nose was removed and three independent sets of motion replaced Gresley's derived valve gear. In order to have connecting rods of the same length for both 'inside' and 'outside' cylinders, the 'outside' cylinders were set back behind the bogie and driven on to the centre coupled axle. The five other locomotives in the P2 Class were converted during 1944 and became Class A2/2. No 2001 'Cock O' the North' is pictured here in 1944 shortly after it was rebuilt. The Thompson locomotives however did not work as well on the Scottish routes as they had done in their previous form and in 1949 were allocated work south of the border.

Thompson's L1 – The first completely new LNER locomotive to appear after the Second World War was Thompson's Class L1 prototype 2-6-4 tank engine No. 9000. It had 5ft 2in driving wheels and was designed for outer suburban work. As the prototype of the Class it was the only one to be built at Doncaster, although 99 were eventually built elsewhere including Darlington Works, The North British Locomotive Company and R Stephenson Hawthorns. The bogie on No. 9000 was similar to that fitted to A1 No. 4470 'Great Northern' which was rebuilt at the Plant about the same time. Almost immediately after its completion No. 9000 began the most extensive trials ever arranged by the LNER for an engine of this type. It was involved in every duty from express passenger work to heavy shunting and this continued until 1947.

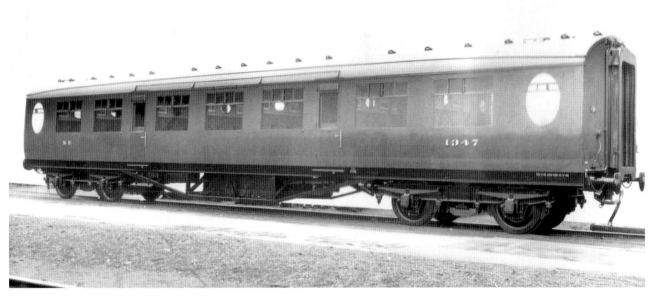

Thompson's Prototype Coaches – Carriage No. 1347, was one of two Thompson designed vehicles that were built at the Plant during 1945. Thompson's vehicles represented a complete break from the Gresley tradition. The carriage's main external difference was the steel panelled sides, although not the first on the LNER, they anticipated the end of the teak panelled bodies of the Gresley era. Other changes included deeper and wider windows, plain roofs of equal profile throughout (instead of drop-end roofs) and oval shaped windows, with white opaque glass in toilet compartments. Apart from these external differences Thompson's designs also featured a revised interior layout. The coaches were divided into sections of two or three compartments separated by transverse vestibules which adjoined the main corridor. This meant that passengers had to walk past no more than one compartment to reach an external door. General production of Thompson's various new designs for standard stock began in the immediate post-war years and many vehicles were allocated to East Coast and other principal workings.

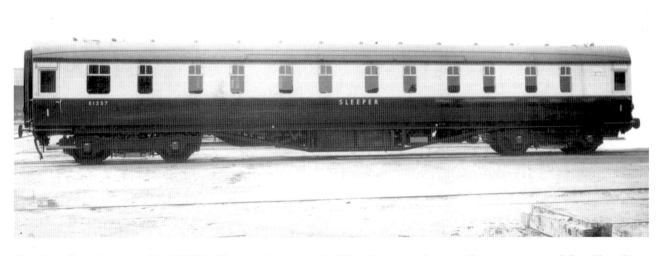

Sleeping Cars-Carriage No. E1257, illustrated in the early BR crimson and cream livery, was one of five First Class Sleeping Cars which were built at the Plant during 1950. The vehicles had steel panelled bodies, an overall length of 66ft 6in, a width of 9ft 2¹/₂ and radiused corners to the body side windows. They were also fitted with pressure ventilation. The interiors consisted of ten convertible berths and an attendant's compartment.

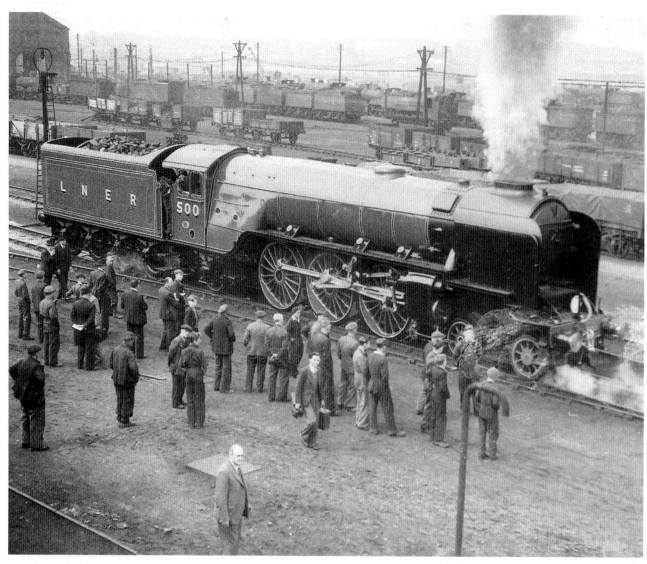

Thompson's A2/3 – Thompson produced four Classes of 'Pacific' locomotives, the A1/1, A2/2 and A2/3. The first two of these Classes were rebuilt from earlier designs but the A2/3 was the result of his search for a standard 'Pacific' locomotive. It had 6ft 2in driving wheels, boiler pressure of 250lb/sq. in. and three 19in x 26 in cylinders. Thirty locomotives were originally ordered from the Plant in 1944, but as Thompson retired in 1946 whilst they were under construction, only 15 were built to his original designs. The first A2/3 No 500 (later 60500) was named Edward Thompson, after its designer, and was the 2000th engine to be built by the Plant. The top and bottom pictures on this page show the loco both with and without its nameplate.

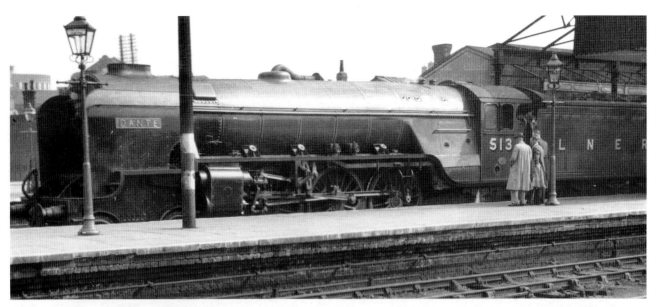

Thompson Class – A2/3 No. 513 'Dante' is seen at Doncaster station on 12th September 1946.

'Great Northern' Rebuilt – Thompson's most blatant act of vindictiveness towards Gresley was judged to be the rebuilding of pioneer 'Pacific' No. 4470 'Great Northern', which was completed by September 1945. The new locomotive had three separate sets of Walschaerts valve gear to replace the conjugated valve gear, a 250lb/sq. in. A4 boiler with a banjo dome, 'outside' cylinders set well back behind the bogie and shortened cab sides. Although the engine looked impressive in its new blue livery with red lining, its overall appearance was ungainly. The locomotive is shown here on 19th September 1945.

Three months after being rebuilt 'Great Northern' underwent a Light Repair at the Plant. It emerged with large smoke deflectors and more conventional lengthened cab sides.

LNER

Peppercorn's A2 – Thompson's retirement from the post of LNER Chief Mechanical Engineer in 1946 brought his unpopular career to an end. He was succeeded by Arthur Henry Peppercorn, who quickly decided that after the first 15 of Thompson's A2/3 'Pacifics' were completed, the remaining engines on order would be built to his own modified design. The first of Peppercorn's engines, No. 525 and named after him appeared from the Plant in December 1947, the last month of the LNER's existence. The locomotives were Classified A2 and one of their main differences with Thompson's engines was a reversion to the orthodox position of the 'outside' cylinders astride the bogie. Thompson's three 19in x 26in cylinders were retained together with the Walschaerts valve gear. No. 525 'A.H. Peppercorn' is pictured with its designer and other members of the Doncaster workforce outside the Crimpsall on 31st December 1947, the last day of the LNER.

An A2 Class engine's boiler in the hydraulic riveter. Photograph taken in the Boiler Shop on 19 November 1947.

A2 Class engine being wheeled in the New Erecting Shop on 15 January 1948.

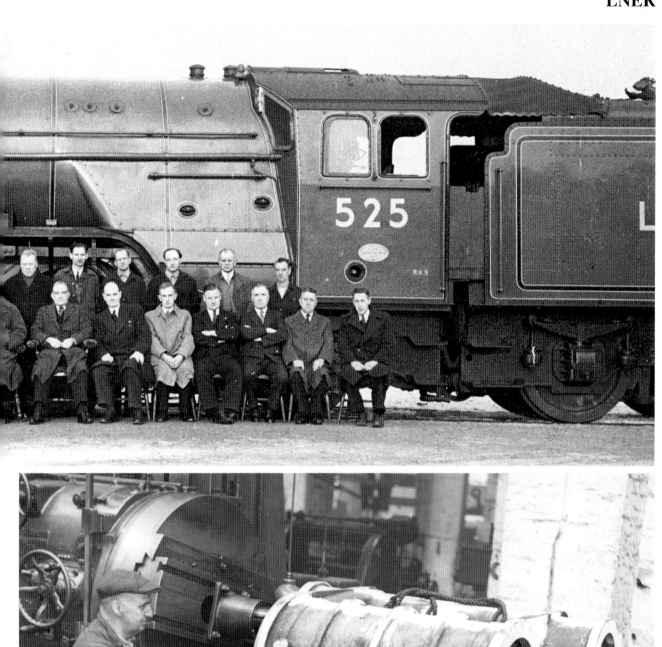

Mr H Stanley Richards working on a cylinder boring machine on 4 October 1945 in the Main Machine (D) shop..

Plant Views – This view taken on 26 March 1946, from the roof of the Power House (adjacent to the Locomotive Paint Shop), shows the main roadway which led into The Plant from the right, and branched off to the various Shops. From left to right the areas adjacent are, the Timber Drying Shed (double-roofed building), Fabrication and Spring Shop (the two buildings in front of the tall chimney) the Grinding, White Metal and Machine Fitters Shop (contained in the building with one large and two small gables) and the Main Machine Shop (former original Erecting Shop) triple roofed building. The two carriages outside the Machine Shop were used as offices for many years.

This view, again taken from the roof of the Power House on 29 March 1946, depicts (from left to right) the Iron Foundry (double gabled building) and the Boiler Shop (the other three buildings). These buildings would later form part of the National Supply Centre (Railpart) in the late 1980's.

GIANTS REFRESHED

"PACIFICS" IN THE L·N·E·R LOCOMOTIVE WORKS, DONCASTER

Giants Refreshed - This photograph, together with another similar view, was taken in the Locomotive Paint Shop on 22nd January 1947. Both pictures were used as a basis for Terence Cuneo's painting 'Giants Refreshed (illustrated here).' Whilst it was true that Class A4 'Merlin' had just been repainted or 'refreshed' in some way, it was not the case with Thompson's A2/3 'Honeyway'. This locomotive had just been built and was having its nameplate fitted for the first time.

This view, from 29th March 1946, is from the Crimpsall roof looking east towards the railway station with the Iron Foundry in the distance and the Weigh House and Paint Shop on the right.

Peppercorn's A1 – Thompson produced various drawings for his proposed standard Class A1s; some were based on his rebuilt 'Great Northern' and others included streamlining. Orders were subsequently placed with Doncaster and Darlington for a total of 39 A1s. However, these engines were not built, because soon after the order was placed Thompson was succeeded by Peppercorn, who produced further drawings for the A1s. The new designs dispensed with the previous proposals for streamlining, but some of Thompson's ideas were retained. These included the divided drive, separate valve gears for each of the three 19in x 26in cylinders and the large redesigned Diagram 118 boiler, which had been fitted to Peppercorn's A2s. A short time before the first A1s were built, it was decided to amend the design further, by replacing the single chimney with a Kylchap double blastpipe and chimney. The first A1 No. 60114 'W P Allen', was built at the Plant, and is pictured here on 18 October 1948. A total of 49 engines appeared between August 1948 and December 1949, 26 from the Plant and 23 from Darlington.

Last Teak Framed Vehicles – 11 Kitchen Cars with anthracite-electric cooking equipment were built at the Plant during 1948/49. They were designed to operate with Open Firsts and Thirds to form a three-car set. The photograph here shows two Kitchen Cars under construction on 25th April 1949. The entire group of vehicles was amongst the last to be built with teak-body framing at the Plant. For a comparison between the construction methods used here and those subsequently employed on all steel-bodied vehicles see page 83. The picture here, taken on 25 April 1949, shows carriage construction restarted in the newly rebuilt Main Carriage Shop.

New Post Office Vehicles – The Plant built several Post Office vehicles during the GNR period, but only produced one Post Office Stowage Van during the LNER era. In 1949/50, six Post Office Sorting Vans were constructed, having a similar layout to a group of LNER Post Office vehicles, which had been built during 1933 at York. The Doncaster-built vans had 8ft 6³/₄ in wide bodies, 60ft underframes and double bolster bogies. Full sorting facilities were provided, but net collection apparatus was omitted. The vehicles were allocated to the Newcastle, Bristol and East Anglian working. This view shows the Plant's Main Carriage Shop 'high bay' on 3 November 1949, with a Post Office Sorting Van aloft.

The First BR Standard Stock – In 1950/1 the Plant built a batch of 10 Kitchen Cars Nos 80000-80009, which were amongst the first British Railway's Standard, all steel vehicles to be produced. The steel bodies were made from five sub-assemblies. The complete set of panels for a coach side were butted together and carbon arc welded, by machine, on a roller table. The steel skin and subframe were clamped together in a main jig and the whole welded together with the panels stitch welded to the frame. The above photograph, taken on 12th December 1950, gives a general view of the Kitchen Car body shell assembly jigs.

Post Office Sorting Van – Interior view of Post Office Sorting Van taken on 7 December 1949.

Plant Centenary Celebrations – The opening ceremony of the Doncaster Locomotive, Carriage and Wagon Works 1953 Centenary Celebrations was undertaken by RA Riddles. It included an exhibition of locomotives, carriages and wagons and was staged over the weekend of 19/20 September 1953. The upper view is from the roof of the Paint Shop and the lower photo is looking towards the Main Machine Shop (original Erecting Shop).

LMS Designed 2-6-0 – The 2-6-0 Class 4F was H.G. Ivatt's, son of HA Ivatt, final design and last locomotive to be introduced by the LMS prior to nationalisation. The Class consisted of 162 engines and a total of 50 were Plant-built between 1950-1952. Class 4F No. 43050 (built at Doncaster) was pictured at the Plant on 11 July 1950.

Standard Tank – Between 1951-1956, 155 Standard Class 4, 2-6-4 Tanks were built for use on mixed-traffic work. The majority were produced at Brighton, but in 1954 the Plant constructed a batch of 10, Nos 80106-80115. No 80108 was photographed on 3rd November 1954.

Standard Class 5 – Following the appointment of RA Riddles as the new British Railways Chief Mechanical and Electrical Engineer, it was proposed to build twelve new types of locomotives to standard designs. The standard Class 5, 4-6-0 mixed traffic locomotive was largely designed at Doncaster and between 1951-1957. A total of 172 engines were built 42 at the Plant and 130 at Derby Works. No 73104 is pictured on 26 September 1955.

BR

Valve Gear Machine – The Plant's Locomotive Drawing Office supplied designs for coupling and connecting rods, valve gear and cylinder details in respect of many of the BR Standard engine types. Two members of the Drawing Office team are seen here on 1 March 1951 plotting valve events on a valve gear design machine.

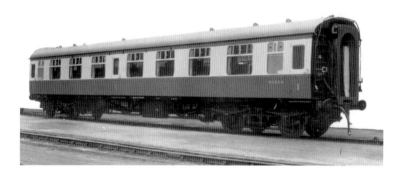

Open First Stock – Between 1951-1954, 20 BR Standard Open First carriages were built at York and the Birmingham Railway Carriage and Wagon Co. Ltd. These vehicles were constructed with end doors only. During 1954-1956, the Plant built a further 60 Open Firsts, with end doors and also centre doors which were cut into the seating bay. Consequently, glazed partitions formed a vestibule across the centre of the coach which had three saloons of 4, 2 and 2 bays. One of the 2 bays was a non-smoking saloon. Fixed seating in the vehicle was arranged two and one each side of an off-central passageway and tables were fitted to each bay of seats. Although the vehicles were not specifically intended as Restaurant Cars they were often used for this purpose and were coupled to Kitchen Cars. Illustrated are the interior and exterior of Open First No. M3024.

Carriage Shop Heating – It was a common practice at The Plant and elsewhere to use redundant locomotive boilers to raise steam for heating purposes. Two Ivatt Atlantics, Nos 3274 and 3285 provide steam heating for the Works' Carriage Shops.

End of the Road – Pioneer Class A4 'Silver Link' stands complete with nameplates on the scrap line, known as 'Burma Road' at The Plant in June/July 1963. Although six

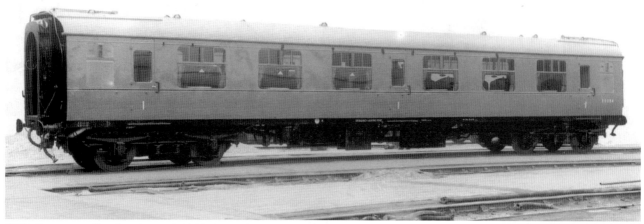

1957 Prototype Stock – Around 1956 the British Transport Commission (BTC) ordered 14 prototype coaches to evaluate and gauge public reaction to the many new ideas that were to be embodied in them. After the BTC had laid down certain specifications and guidelines, eight vehicles were built by four outside firms and the remaining six at the Plant, the only BR workshop involved with the project. Four of the Plant's six vehicles were newly built, the other two were refitted standard stock. An external feature of the vehicle was that its side profile was flat from the waist to the cantrail. The interior had fixed seating, arranged in six bays, divided into two saloons. The seats, which were designed to resemble individual chairs, were low backed and arranged around tables. Space was provided between the backs of chairs to accommodate hand luggage. The lighting was provided by a combination of fluorescent tubes, above the passageway and incandescent lamps, suspended from the luggage rack over each table. When all the 14 prototypes were in service, they were monitored and passengers travelling in them were questioned about the various modifications and features. Unfortunately the overall project was largely a failure. This was mainly because the consequences of improving vehicles' interiors, within the basic Mark 1 body shell, naturally led to fewer seats and a weight increase. These disadvantages could not be outweighed by the improved facilities offered to passengers and as a result these prototypes had little direct influence on later stock.

Modernisation Begins – In the British Transport Commission's Modernisation Plan it was announced that over the next five to ten years diesel rail traction would replace steam engines. As British Railways acknowledged the fact that private diesel manufacturers had more expertise with construction work than their own workshops, various companies were contracted to provide locomotives. Brush Ltd, at Loughborough, received an order during 1955, for 20 diesel-electric locomotives of 1, 250 hp. The first one D5500 constructed during 1957 had a Mirrlees V-type 12 cylinder engine and an A1A-A1A bogie layout. This later feature meant that only the 'outer' and 'inner' axle on each bogie was powered, leaving a 'pony' set of wheels in the centre. The first 20 locomotives proved to be successful and further orders were placed. By 1962 a total of 263 locomotives, belonging to Classes 30 and 31 were produced. The Plant has had a long association with these locomotives, being responsible in the early years for 'accepting' them on behalf of British Railways and implementing a variety of modifications as well as carrying out heavy overhauls in subsequent years. In this picture Class 31s can be seen in 2-Bay of the Crimpsall during 1966 whilst being re-engineered with English Electric units.

Shunter Construction – Between 1952-1962 various BR workshops built over 1000 0-6-0 diesel-electric shunters, which became the country's largest fleet of locomotives. The shunters were based on various LMS prototypes, constructed before and after the Second World War. The same basic body design was used for all the Classes but various technical differences existed within each type. During 1957-58 the Plant completed 30 0-6-0 shunters, Nos D3497-3502 (DEJ5), D3608-3611, D3652-3664, D3680-3686 (DEJ4 later Class 08). This picture shows Class 08 construction in the New Erecting Shop during 1959.

Acceptance Trials – The 1965 Modernisation Plan proposed that new locomotives should be built in five different power groups, Type 1 (up to 1,000 hp), Type 2 (1,001-1,500 hp), Type 3 (1,501-1,999 hp), Type 4 (2,000-2,999 hp), Type 5 (3,000hp and above). During the 1950s and 1960s the Plant carried out 'acceptance' trials on a number of these types. Pioneer Type 3 Class 37 No D6700 is now preserved in the National Railway Museum.

Type 2 – An exterior view of main-line Diesel-Electric Loco (North British Type 2) D 6102 taken at The Plant December 1958.

Type 4 – In December 1955 the first of several orders was placed with the English Electric Company Ltd to design and construct locomotives in the Type 4 power range. Initially 10 locomotives were built for use on Class 1 passenger and fast long-distance freight traffic. The new locomotives were completed during 1958 and the Plant carried out 'acceptance' trials on a number of them. By 1962 there were 199 of this kind of Type 4 in existence and under BR diesel locomotive classification they all became Class 40. The first of its Class No. D200 is pictured here on 24 March 1958.

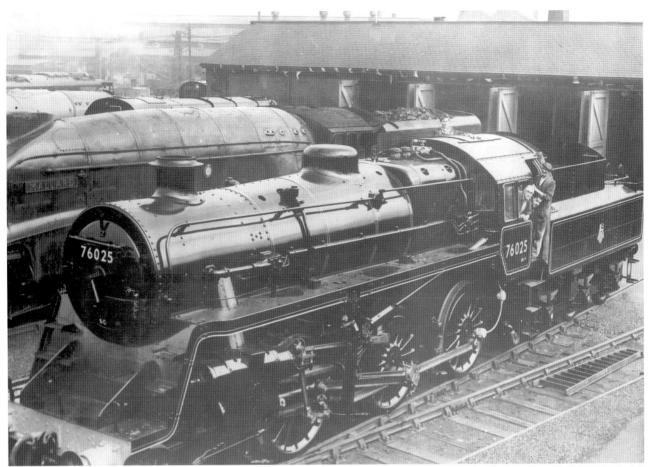

End of Steam – Most of the design work for the Standard Class 4, 2-6-0 locomotive, probably based on H G Ivatt's, 2-6-0 design for the LMS in 1947, was carried out at Doncaster. Construction of the 115 locomotives, Nos 76000-76114, during 1952-57, was divided between Horwich (45) and Doncaster (70). The engine had 5ft 3 in. coupled wheels and 17½ x 26 in. cylinders. Boiler pressure was 225 lb/sq. in. and many of the locomotives were fitted with small B.R. 2A, 3,500 gallon/6 ton capacity tenders. No. 76114 was the last of 2,228 steam locomotives to be built at Doncaster. Earlier Class member No. 76025 is seen outside the Paint Shop.

Type 2 Locomotives – Several different builders were awarded contracts for Type 2 locomotives under the Modernisation Programme. In 1958/9 the Birmingham Carriage and Wagon Company Ltd completed an order for 20 locomotives, numbered D5300-D5319. These locomotives were initially employed on many King's Cross suburban duties as well as on selected main-line routes. After this time the fleet was allocated to Scotland. A further 27 locomotives numbered D5320-D5346, which had been built in 1959, were also allocated to Scotland. Both groups of locomotives eventually became Class 26. D5415 is pictured on 27 September 1962.

AC Electric Prototypes – The introduction of AC electrification was included in the BTC's Modernisation programme. First it was decided to electrify the London Midland Region West Coast route from London to Birmingham, Liverpool and Manchester and build 100 prototype AC electric locomotives. All AC electric locomotives had to include standardised methods of driving and uniform control layouts in all the cabs. Also, before production began, a number of stipulations were made regarding mechanical proportions, the axle load and body shape. Building the 100 prototypes was divided between five manufacturers with 60 being constructed by private contractors and 40 by BR workshops. The latter batch was originally intended to be produced, in equal proportions, at Crewe and Doncaster, but in the event all (Nos E3056-E3095) were built at the Plant between 1961-1964. The 100 prototypes, after completion, were grouped into five classes AL1-5. The Doncaster locomotives, Class AL5 (later Class 85) unlike locomotives in other Classes, were fitted with semi-conductor rectifiers and rheostatic braking. An AL5 locomotive is shown here under construction in the New Erecting Shop and newly outshopped first of the Class No E3056 stands in the Plant Yard following completion.

Carriage & Wagon Design – View in the Carriage & Wagon Drawing Office on 26 April 1961. This area was originally the 1853 Upper Turnery converted in 1935 to a Central Carriage and Wagon design office for the LNER.

Electric Multiple Units – To cater for the Eastern Region's electric services between Liverpool Street and Chingford, Enfield Town, Hertford East and Bishops Stortford, 71 multiple unit sets were introduced during 1960. There were 52 three-car sets which were built at York and 19 four car sets produced at Doncaster. The latter group, however had bogies supplied from York, while the General Electric Co. Ltd provided the electrical equipment for both sets of vehicles. The Doncaster batch Class 305/2 comprised a Driving Trailer with saloon and compartment accommodation, a Motor Coach, a Trailer Coach and another Driving Trailer. The improved external appearance of the front and reverse of the vehicles, in comparison with the Class 302 units, was the result of the influence of the BTC's Design Panel. The photograph shows the last set of 305/2 vehicles built at the Plant, on 18th November 1960.

Deltic cab – Interior view of Deltic cab D9001, taken on 2 March 1961.

Southern Electrics – Following the decision by the Southern Region, to electrify the Kent Coast main-lines, at the increased rail voltage of 750V DC, as part of the 1955 BTC Modernisation Plan, an order was placed with The Plant, in the late 1950s, for 24 booster electric locomotives Nos E5000-E5023. The locomotives were capable of operating by third (live) rail or overhead current collection and were used to haul freight and passenger trains such as the 'Golden Arrow' and 'Night Ferry' services. When working in goods yards and sidings the locomotives mainly operated by overhead power since the presence of a third (live) rail in these areas would have been a danger to personnel working at ground level. During 1966/7, 10 of the Class were converted, at Crewe Works, to electro-diesel locomotives becoming Class 74, Nos 74001-74010. The remainder became Class 71 and were numbered, 71001-71014. Both classes were withdrawn by 1977. Eight locomotives were dismantled at Doncaster. E5001 is preserved at the National Railway Museum, York.

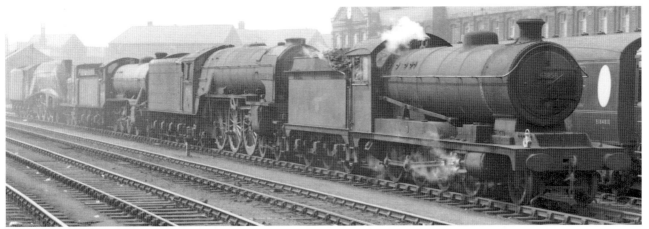

Awaiting repairs – Steam locomotives awaiting repair near Denison House, with 63858 heading the line and Class A1 locomotive 'Hal o' the Wynd' just behind.

45T crane – The Doncaster Motive Power Depot's 45T crane is seen here working at the Plant during April 1952.

In the Crimpsall – 2-bay in the Crimpsall with locomotives 60532 (left) and 60046 undergoing general repair.

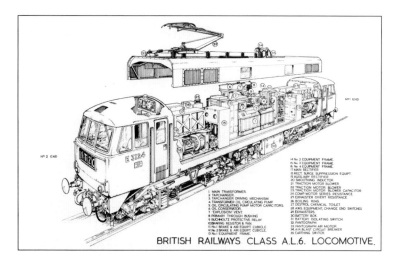

BRITISH RAILWAYS CLASS A.L.6. LOCOMOTIVE.

AL6 Production – Much information was gained from the five Classes of prototype AC electric locomotives when they were in operation and this led to a production batch of 100 locomotives being built in 1965-66. These became Class AL6 (later Class 86) and Nos E3101-E3140 were constructed by the Plant and Nos E3141-E3200 by the English Electric Co. Ltd at the Vulcan Foundry. The locomotive's design was similar to the two Classes AL1/AL5 and the superstructure, except for a slightly different shaped front, resembled the AL5. The layout of equipment was modified and only one pantograph was fitted; two had originally been used on the prototype Classes. The locomotives were also at least two feet longer than their predecessors which helped to give a better interior layout for maintenance purposes. The addition of axlehung motors unfortunately gave the locomotives poor riding qualities. As a result of much experimentation by the Derby research team to overcome the problem, the Flexicoil Suspension system was in due course adopted in a major portion of the fleet. Several members of the Class were used during the early 1970s, in experiments for producing a further improvement in the overall design. This resulted in the introduction of the powerful Class 87s in 1973. The middle photograph shows Class 86 locomotives under construction on 3rd November 1964. The lower photograph is of members of the Locomotive Drawing Office taken in the Locomotive Plant Shop on 17th January 1966, alongside the last locomotive of the series.

Wagon Light Repair Shop – This Shop was established during 1964/5 in the area formerly occupied by the Carriage Paint Shop. The new Shop consisted of six roads to enable wagon light repairs to be undertaken on a progressive system. Traversers at each end of the Shop allowed the inward and outward movement of wagons. An electrically operated unit was used to lift the vehicles when wheels needed to be changes, axleboxes reconditioned and bearings fitted. This view of the traverser in the Wagon Light Repair Shop was taken during March 1966.

Wagon Heavy Repairs Shop – Carriage building and classified carriage repairs ceased at the Plant following the implementation of BR's 1962 Re-organisation of Workshops Plan. By 1965 the Main Carriage Shop had been converted for Wagon Repair Work, which had been transferred from the workshops at the Carr. The view depicted here on 25 April 1966 shows the Wagon Heavy Repair Shop which was formerly a section of the Main Carriage Shop. The Heavy Shop consisted of three main bays, and the heavy repair of Brake Vans, Covered Goods and Open Wagons was undertaken on a progressive system. Traversers were provided at both ends of the Shop to facilitate the movement of wagons. The centre bay was the main bay for the removal and replacement of wheels and axleboxes and elevated platforms were provided for painting purposes. At the south end of the Shop provision was made for the renovation of wheels, axles, axleboxes and bearings.

The 'Deltics' – Following the success of the 'Deltic' prototype, which underwent rigorous tests on various areas of the rail network during the late 1950s, the BTC placed an order with the English Electric Company Ltd to manufacture 22 similar locomotives. On completion the Plant carried out 'acceptance' trials on the locomotives and subsequently overhauled them once they were in service. Two Napier D18/25 'Deltic' engines were fitted in each locomotive and when operating together gave a total output of 3,300 hp. The 'Deltic' fleet conformed to the British Railways Type 5 power classification and was introduced on East Coast main-line services during the early, 1960s, to replace the A1, A2, A3 and A4 Classes of steam engines. 'Deltic' No. D9019 'Royal Highland Fusilier' is illustrated above, in 1963 undergoing a power unit change in the Crimpsall and in the Test House during 1965.

Last Steam Locomotive Repair – Officially, A4 No.60009 'Union of South Africa' was the last steam locomotive to undergo an overhaul at the Plant. On the day the engine returned to service, 6 November 1963, it was photographed with several groups of Plant staff. Despite this, it was rumoured amongst the staff that a War Department Austerity 2-8-0 was really the Plant last steam repair and the honour of this event was not allowed to fall on such an undistinguished engine. However, it was estimated that between 1853-1963 around 40, 000 steam locomotives were overhauled and repaired at the Plant. No. 60009, following withdrawal in June 1966, was preserved by the Lochty Private Railway Company.

'Mallard' Preserved – Apart from No 4469 'Ralph Wedgwood', which was scrapped in 1942 following bomb damage, the entire fleet of 34 A4 locomotives was withdrawn between December 1962 and September 1966. Six were preserved and included amongst these was No. 4468 'Mallard', the holder of the world speed record for steam traction. Following withdrawal in April 1963 this locomotive was overhauled at the Plant and is seen here on 27 November 1963. On completion it was stored for a short period at Nine Elms Yard, South London, before being delivered to the British Transport Museum at Clapham during the night of 29 February/1st March 1964. However, following the establishment of the National Railway Museum, York in 1975 the locomotive was transferred there.

Frost precautions – The severe winter of 1963-4 brought havoc to the railways, immobilising many steam and diesel locomotives. Throughout the remainder of 1964, the Plant modified a large number of diesel locomotives in an attempt to protect them from extreme weather conditions. The programme of work was called the 'Frost Precautions' and included installing steam heating in radiator compartments as well as lagging all external and internal water and air pipes. Network analysis techniques, manning charts and other productivity measures, were used in planning the operations and as a result it was possible to bring locomotives into the Plant on a Friday night and despatch them back into service by Sunday. Initially eight locomotives were dealt with each weekend and this was gradually increased, as the staff gained experience to a maximum of 12. The Class 31 locomotives were involved in the 'Frost Precautions' and several members of the Class can be seen undergoing modification in 4-bay of the Crimpsall Repair Shop during May 1964.

Diesel Multiple Unit Repairs – Although the Plant was not responsible for building any of the DMUs during their introduction in the 1950s, it has nevertheless, undertaken repairs on virtually all the different Classes. Much of this work was carried out in the West Carriage Shop (becoming known as the DMU Repair Shop from the early 1960s) and the North Carriage Shed. On arrival at the Plant for repair a DMU was taken into a washing pit, outside the Repair Shop, where the underframe was washed. Once in the Repair Shop, the DMU body was lifted off the bogies and passed down a repair line. The bogies, meanwhile were transferred to a separate bay for cleaning and repair. The machine and fitting sections in the D.M.U. Repair Shop maintained the various components including gearboxes and final drives. Facilities were also available for wheel turning, balancing and ultrasonic flaw detection. Another section was responsible for the repair of all electrical equipment. There was also a bay which was used for painting and 'finishing' the vehicles. DMU work in the North Carriage Shed included repairs to damaged vehicles as well as sheet-metal work, plumbing, brass finishing and chromium plating. The picture here shows the DMU Shop's North End traverser in April 1966.

London Transport Battery Locomotives – During 1973/74 the Plant made a departure from more conventional locomotive construction when 11 battery locomotives Nos L44-L54 were built for London Transport. The locomotives were similar to previous service stock designs, with driving cabs at each end and incorporating the same dimensions as tube stock. Each vehicle was able to operate independently on their own batteries or from 600V DC fourth rail supply. At the time of their introduction the locomotives were intended for hauling engineering trains during the construction of the Fleet (Jubilee) Line and the Piccadilly Line extension to Heathrow Central.

Bridge Construction – Under BREL, main Works were able to bid for private sector work including non-railway based contracts. Here in the New Erecting Shops in c1971 bridge girders are under fabrication.

BREL

Northern Ireland Railways – In 1969 Hunslet Engineering Co. Ltd won an order from Northern Ireland Railways, despite fierce US competition, for three 1,350 hp diesel-electric locomotives. The deadline for the delivery of the first locomotive was only ten months. This was a formidable task for Hunslet, since their locomotive production capacity was fully occupied with home and overseas orders. Consequently, Hunslet approached the Plant for assistance. The latter agreed to fabricate the superstructure, assemble the equipment, then test and finally paint the finished locomotives. English Electric-AEI. Traction provided much of the basic design and supplied the power equipment (many components were common with those already used on the diesel-electrics in service with NIR). Hunslet acted as the main co-ordinator of the exercise, as well as the main contractor, undertaking the detail design work on the superstructure and the bogies, which they also manufactured. As a result of the combined efforts of the three parties the first was completed in May 1970, which met the specified deadline. On completion the locomotives were transported by road from the Plant, before being shipped to Northern Ireland. The locomotives operated on the non-stop 'Enterprise Express' trains between Belfast and Dublin, a journey of 113 miles, which was scheduled to take two hours.

'Blue Peter' Preserved – Peppercorn Class A2 60532 'Blue Peter' was withdrawn from service on 31st December 1966 following a working life of just eighteen and a half years. On 29th March 1968, after being stored at Thornton shed in Scotland, it was sold to Geoffrey Drury and Brian Hollingsworth who established a 'Blue Peter' Locomotive Society. One of the Society's aims was to raise funds for the locomotive's restoration. An appeal brought a response from over 3,000 people and owed much to the publicity received from the BBC Television children's programme of the same name, which on several occasions featured the locomotive. As a result of the appeal 'Blue Peter' entered the Plant in May 1969 for a light overhaul and repainting. On completion there was a large public renaming ceremony at the Plant on 22nd November 1970. Once the excitement of this event had subsided the locomotive's newly restored appearance began to cause some controversy. This was because it had several features (LNER on the tender and No. 532 on the cab sides) which it had not carried whilst the locomotive was in service. The locomotive is the only Peppercorn 'Pacific' to have survived.

Battery Locomotive conversions - In 1975 and 1980 the Plant converted eight Class 501 EMU Driving Cars into battery/electric locomotives. They were intended to be used by the Electrical Engineer's department, primarily in areas of restricted tunnel lines. Each vehicle was rebuilt with a 'flat top' to enable staff to deal with overhead repairs. Car No. 97703 is pictured here during January 1980.

The Queen at the Plant – Her Majesty Queen Elizabeth II and HRH the Duke of Edinburgh are pictured on a visit to the Plant on 29 July 1975. The middle photograph is taken in the Apprentice Training School and the lower picture is in No 4 Bay (east) in the Crimpsall.

BREL

Apprentice Training School – Photographed outside the 1853 Turneries Building (now Denison House) apprentices and instr

Apprentice Training School – A view in the Apprentice Training School shortly after opening in August 1965.

or the camera in August 1978.

Doncaster's First Class 56 – In the mid 1970s the Class 56 locomotive was designed to meet BR's need for a new heavy freight locomotive. Nos 56001-56030 were built by a Romanian company Electropute of Craiova. The company had won the order because it had assured early delivery of the locomotives. Unfortunately, the locomotives proved to be of an inferior quality and much modification work needed to be carried out in British workshops before they were fully operational on BR. Construction of a further batch of locomotives was subsequently undertaken at the Plant; the first locomotive No. 56031 being completed during April 1977. Although Doncaster had excellent facilities for the fabrication of the locomotive's structure, there was insufficient skilled staff to manufacture all the fabrications required. To solve this problem a number of components were manufactured at other BRE L Works and then assembled at Doncaster on the locomotive. A total of 85 Class 56 locomotives were produced at Doncaster before the work was transferred to Crewe. This enabled Doncaster to concentrate on building the Class 58 locomotive. The lower picture was taken on 5 April 1977, when the locomotive was 'handed over' to British Rail.

Cement vehicle – A Ketton Cement vehicle outside E2 Shop during September 1975.

Crane Repairs – After undergoing repairs a mobile crane is parked outside E2 Shop during 1972.

Soda Ash Vehicle – A wagon (tank) being fabricated for a soda ash vehicle. The picture was taken on 21 May 1974.

BREL

'Deltics' – The End of the Line – Withdrawal of the 'Deltic' fleet began in January 1980 and was completed by January 1982. Six locomotives were preserved whilst the remaining 16 in the Class were dismantled at the Plant. In the top picture No 55018 'Ballymoss' meets its fate during January 1982.

Deltic Dismantled – Deltic 55021 seen partially dismantled during 1982

A line of Deltics awaiting the cutter's torch in 1982.

Class 58 Construction – The Class 58 locomotive was the result of an attempt to design an engine that was cheaper to build and easier to maintain than the Class 56. It was also hoped that the new locomotive could be suitably adapted for export. The main difference between the Class 56 and 58 was that the latter had a non-load bearing superstructure. All major items in the 58 locomotive such as cabs and cooler groups were produced as complete units or modules and bolted to a rigid under-frame. This not only reduced costly time spent in the Erecting Shop, but also subsequent maintenance costs. Additionally the absence of a body shell in preference for a simple superstructure with access doors was much more convenient for maintenance staff when removing the module equipment.

As it was intended to build the locomotives at Doncaster, members of the Plant staff and the Development Engineer and Design Department at Derby formed a close liaison throughout the initial development stages. The first Class 58 locomotive No 58001 emerged from the Plant in 1982 and a total of 50 were produced.

British Rail Maintenance Limited

General Repairs – Brush locomotive No. 31235 photographed in the Crimpsall during the late 1980s after undergoing a General Repair. The picture was taken whilst brake testing was being carried out with Shift Supervisor Dave McArdle third from the right.

CEM Repair – A Cost Effective Maintenance repair is being carried out on a Class 47 locomotive during the late 1980s in the Crimpsall's 4-Bay.

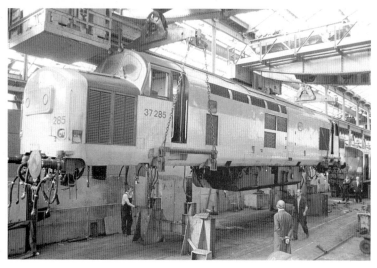

CEM Repair – After undergoing a CEM repair Class 37 locomotive No. 37 285, resplendent in freight livery, is being lifted in preparation to being placed on replacement bogies.

An old generation 'Heritage' DMU has undergone a C3 repair and the painters are seen here applying a coat of undercoat in the Crimpsall. A C3 repair would include attention to bogies, brakes as well as doors and locks and a vehicle repaint.

Test House – A scene in the Test House where Class 31 locomotive 31 282 is receiving a final, static test prior to a trial run.

Trailer Car – A DMU Trailer Car is being lifted to its bogies in the Crimpsall after receiving a Classified Repair.

BRML

Class 365 Completion – Completion of the Class 365 EMU's, begun at York, was undertaken in the former Power Unit Shop at Doncaster. The photograph was taken on 29 September 1996.

Fitting Decals – Melvin Hodgkinson is seen fitting decals to a Mainline Freight Class 58 locomotive in January 1996.

1994 Open Weekend – A busy scene at the BRML Open Weekend held in 1994. The event was held in conjunction with the town's 800th Charter celebrations.

National Supply Centre – The site separation works enabling the formation of the National Supply Centre required significant alterations to many utilities and services that had previously been common across The Plant site. One of the most significant of these concerned the Central Power House, which was located on the site of the original Forge of 1866, which itself had been demolished in 1965. The Power House supplied distributed steam for heating and other processes throughout the Works, and was replaced by a number of new smaller boiler houses and heating systems, including one using ducted air in the Crimpsall Shop. The completion of these works enabled the demolition of the Power House to proceed in July 1987, clearing the way for the extension of the new access road to the NSC Main Warehouse (former West Carriage Shop). This photograph taken on 2nd January 1987 shows the completed first section of the access road leading to the three chimneys of the Power House, situated between the Boiler Shop (1882) to the left and New Erecting Shop (1891) to the right. The road would eventually lead to the Loading Bay of the NSC Main Warehouse situated behind the New Erecting Shop.

Access Road to NSC – This photo from October 1986 shows the preparation work for the new access road to the NSC. To the left stands the 1866 Brass Foundry buildings from which a number of lean-to structures used for brass storage (part of No 8 stores) are in the course of being demolished. In the distance partly obscured by the gantry stands The Plant Hotel on Hexthorpe Road. The separate building in the centre distance originally comprised a gatehouse and an earlier police booth and will shortly be demolished to provide room for the new roadway. Behind the twin gable ends to the right (part of the suite of buildings comprising the 1882 Stores) was the Damper Shop (relocated into the RFS site) and beyond that were originally stables for horses used to shunt railway vehicles and pull the Works' fire engine.

NSC – Railpart

DMU Repair Shop – Taken inside the DMU Repair Shop (West Carriage Shop) on 26th November 1986, showing the extensive work required to make the area fit for its new role as the Main Warehouse of the NSC. Showing two of the 'high bay' areas of the Shop, the roof is obscured by the under-hanging scaffold and working platforms whilst a major renovation and painting of the roof was in progress. The Shop cranes (one seen in the distance) were removed and the whole floor area was concreted over, raising the floor level by approximately nine inches.

A Scene Transformed – This photograph taken just over 5 week later on 2nd January 1987 shows the opposite side of the Main Warehouse with refurbished roof, new lighting, repaired downspouts and with the new concrete floor laid. Extensive storage racking is being assembled, which in the 'high bays' extends to the full height of the roofline.

National Supply Centre – 3rd April 1987 and the first parts are being moved into the storage in the National Supply Centre Main Warehouse.

North Carriage Shed, Before and After – From the earliest days of the National Supply Centre it became clear that the amount of material to be stored would soon overwhelm the available warehouse space. The North Carriage Shed stood at the northernmost end of The Plant had also been used as a brass shop, supplying brass and aluminium carriage and DMU fittings such as luggage racks, and containing chrome-plating baths. Plans were soon put in hand to convert the redundant shed to additional warehousing for slower moving stocks. This included an internal refurbishment, redecoration and the laying of a new concrete floor. The first photograph shows the North Carriage Shed on 25th June 1987 with some initial ground works underway, and the second taken just over three months later on 30th September shows the completed refurbishment with new racking already in place on some roads and various materials awaiting storage.

Site Preparation Works – Taken from the roof of the New Erecting Shop looking south showing the extensive track replacement and simplification undertaken as part of the site separation works during 1987. To the right can be seen, the new access road to the National Supply Centre, and to the right of the road in the distance the 1882 Stores building (all now within the Railpart facility). To the left of the road stands the RFS site, with the 1866 Brass Foundry buildings in the distance and to the extreme left of the tracks the gable ends of the 1866 extension to the original Locomotive Erecting Shop, including the large arched window where the steam traverser would enter the Shop.

NSC – Railpart

Sir Robert Reid – Chairman of the British Railways Board, Sir Robert Reid, unveiling a commemorative plaque on the official opening of the NSC on 13th January 1988. An earlier official visit of senior BRB managers planned for 16th October 1987 was disrupted due to the infamous autumn hurricanes that swept across Britain that year.

Main Warehouse – Sir Robert accompanied by David Blake (right), Director of Mechanical & Electrical Engineering, British Railways Board, and Bill Gilbert (left) Materials Manager survey the new Loading Dock of the Main Warehouse at the National Supply Centre on 13th January 1987. This area originally held two large gasholders of the 1866 Gas Works, and in later years was the site of a carriage traverser that ran across the face of the former West Carriage Shop (later DMU Repair Shop).

Main Warehouse – Sir Robert Reid and party survey the storage and retrieval of materials by special 'Rotareach' high level side-loading fork lift trucks from the extensive racking that fills the Main Warehouse of the National Supply Centre.

Bombardier Transportation

The Bombardier Transportation Site – Including the Crimpsall Repair shop in the background.

Testing the Safeset Modification – The Class 91 locomotive is one of the most powerful four axle electric locomotives operating at speeds of up to 125 mph. Power is delivered to the wheels by four body-mounted traction motors each driving a short cardan (propeller) shaft to a substantial bevel-drive gearbox mounted on each axle. Part of the Heavy General Repair programme has concentrated on improving the performance and reliability of the locomotive drive system, including the standardisation of the drive gearbox from two types to one, and the purchase of new gearboxes. To aid the early detection of potential gearbox failure an additional piece of equipment has been installed in the drive system. Named 'Safeset' it automatically disengages the traction drive and provides a failure indication to the driver. Here Chris Harrison tests the 'Safeset' modification following installation at Heavy General Repair. One of the large traction motors can be seen suspended at an angle under the locomotive (to the right of the vehicle stand).

Bombardier Transportation

Mid-life Refurbishment – Between 2000 and 2003, Adtranz (now Bombardier) have undertaken a major mid-life refurbishment and modification of the 31 Class 91 locomotives operated by GNER. Classified as a Heavy General Repair, the overhauled and improved locomotives are renumbered from their original 91000 series to the 91100 range. Here locomotive 91014 St Mungo Cathedral (to be renumbered 91114 on completion) receives attention from Tony Smith in the foreground with Pete Buxton and Trevor Thompson behind. Tony is preparing the outer casing of a Class 91 headlight cover for modification including the fitting of stainless steel covers and new perspex bezels. 91014 was the last of the Class 91 fleet to undergo Heavy General Repair at The Plant.

Doncaster Signing – The Doncaster Works site of Bombardier Transportation Systems provides Class 91 light maintenance services under a 5-year contract with locomotive owners HSBC Rail. In 2003 the contract was signed at a special ceremony at The Plant, where Bombardier's Andrew Lezala (left, President, Service Division) is being congratulated by Bob Marrill of HSBC Rail, accompanied by Doncaster MP, Rosie Winterton, and HSBC's John Reddyhoff. The group are photographed in 4 Bay of the Crimpsall Repair Shop with the entire Doncaster Class 91 team and locomotive 91114, the last of the fleet to receive a Heavy General Repair.

Angel Trains – In 2001 Bombardier Transportation Systems' Doncaster facility was successful in being awarded a contract by GNER for their fleet of High Speed Train (HST) Power Cars owned by Angel Trains. The contract includes the complete rewire of the Power Car in conjunction with other modification and examination work. The photograph shows Chris Harle, Gordon Shakespeare, Gary Temporal and Pete Buxton removing the high-impact resistant cab window from a Class 43 HST Power Car number 43111 in the Crimpsall Repair Shop. On these vehicles the cab is a modular unit constructed of an inner and outer skin of glass reinforced plastic surrounding an inner sandwich of impact absorbent foam, and is removed from the vehicle to facilitate the rewiring operation.

HST Rewiring – Taken inside GNER HST Power Car 43111, the photograph shows Jonathon Warnes and Graham Ellwood (in the foreground) and Ian Wright (at the rear) at work on rewiring and modification work. A new 'Inergen' fire system will be installed and the electrical cubicle has been removed and sent to Bombardier at Crewe for rewiring and re-identification of cables. The rewiring will often coincide with other major work including an 18-month overhaul of the power unit and modification to single-bank firing when idling for long periods. Other attention includes the radiator cooler group with improvements to the security of coolant joints, and more recent work has seen the installation of Wabtec's Q-Tron 'black box' data recorders. The removal of the power unit, cooler group and electrical cubicle greatly assists in accessing the electrical cabling. Here covers have been removed from the trunking which runs horizontally through the vehicle at cant rail (shoulder) height and carries cabling for the auxiliary circuits. A number of new main power cables are visible held in cleats at the edge of the roof opening, their ends hanging loose awaiting termination into junction boxes.

RFS Industries

Mark 3 Driving Van Trailer (DVT) – In the earliest days of RFS in 1987, the company was contracted to undertake bodywork modifications to a Driving Van Trailer (DVT) bodyshell. The DVT was designed to enable conventional loco-hauled passenger trains to work as fixed formation 'push-pull' sets, with the locomotive remaining at one end of the train and the DVT at the other. In the photograph the DVT bodyshell is in No 6 bay of 'D' Shop as George Hyde (left) and Mick Carroll scrutinise the vehicle drawings. The east end of D6 bay is one of the original Locomotive Erecting Shop bays built in 1853. 100 years earlier would have seen Stirling designed engines under manufacture and repair in this bay, with the locomotive berths running at right angles across the shop, in line with the arches on the right, beyond which stood the steam traverser for moving locomotives up and down the length of the Shop.

Channel Tunnel Bogie Test Vehicles – During the construction of the Channel Tunnel in the late 1980's RFS were successful in winning a variety of work with a number of companies involved in the project. Two vehicles were constructed by RFS at Doncaster Works in 1989 for Trans Manche Link (TML), for the purpose of bogie testing. With bodywork built to the Channel Tunnel loading gauge, the vehicle could be fitted with various prototype bogie types for static and dynamic testing and evaluation. Here Channel Tunnel Bogie Test Vehicle 002 leaves the Works entrance on Hexthorpe Road past The Plant Hotel on a low-loader with police escort in June 1989 heading for France.

Schering Weed Killing Train – During 1988 to 1989 RFS converted four Mark 1 passenger coaches and 3 TTA-type tank wagons to form a weed killing train for Schering. Each coach was converted to a particular use; this included a Spray Coach with an end control cab, dosing pumps and external spray nozzles. A Mess-Workshop Coach was fully equipped with a kitchen area, including cookers, microwave, sink, washing machine, adjacent mess area and a separate workshop. A Storage Coach contained a 70 kVA diesel generator to provide all the train auxiliary power and a Dormitory Coach comprised seven sleeping compartments and bathroom facilities. The tank wagons were converted for the storage of water used in the weed spraying operation. The group photograph shows members of the RFS vehicles division involved in the conversion work in April 1989.

TML Challenger Locomotives – RFS secured further work in connection with the Channel Tunnel construction with an order from Trans Manche Link for seven narrow gauge contractors' locomotives to work on tunnelling operations. The locomotives bore the 'Challenger' name and their manufacture was undertaken at Doncaster Works in the old Erecting (D) Shop during 1990 with final assembly work at the former Thomas Hill, Kilnhurst Works. The photograph shows members of the locomotive team with one of the 'Challengers' outside D6 bay at Doncaster Works. Further locomotive work would also follow with the supply of twenty Class 20 to CTTG (Channel Tunnel Trackwork Group) for use on track construction duties in the tunnel.

RFS Industries

Prototype Steel Coil Carriers – A number of significant freight vehicle designs were to emerge from RFS during the period 1990-1991. In addition to twenty six 90-tonne aggregate hoppers built for RMC, the company also produced a prototype series of twelve 90-tonne Railfreight Metals covered steel coil carriers in 1990. Manufactured as groups of 4 vehicles in 3 different vehicle lengths (13, 16 & 19 metres), and classified as types BGA Nos 961000-961003, BHA 962000-962003 and BJA 963000-963003 they were equipped with a retractable hood to protect the finished steel product when in transit. The 19 metre vehicles were designed to transport flat steel on a single spine structure whilst the shorter length vehicles also incorporated removable floor panels underneath which a well structure permitted the transport of coil steel. The vehicles were designed and registered to work in both the UK and in Europe under 'UIC' regulations. Here newly completed BJA-type No 963002 stands at the Works in September 1990.

LUL C Stock – The most significant vehicle contract undertaken by RFS during its life was the refurbishment of London Underground (LUL) C-Stock used on the Circle, District and Hammersmith lines. Undertaken between 1898 and 1993 the work represented a diversification by RFS away from its heavy dependence upon BR and entailed a significant internal refurbishment including new interior finishes, seats and the opening up of new windows in the intermediate vehicle ends, giving improved visibility and passenger security. The scope of work also extended to the design and manufacture of new bogies for the fleet. One of the most visible outward changes was· the painting of the vehicles in a red, white and blue livery in place of the original unpainted aluminium finish, which had become prone to vandalism and graffiti. The work was undertaken across the RFS site including bodywork in the New Erecting (E) Shop, where the upper photograph shows a motor coach being lifted, and the Light Shop where much interior work was done. The group photograph of RFS staff involved in the refurbishment work is taken outside the Paint Shop located between the Light Shop and 'E' Shop. Upon the sale of RFS' passenger business during receivership in 1994, this paint facility was dismantled and moved to Bombardier's site in Horbury, Wakefield.

Fleetcare Redland – One of the early success stories of RFS was the establishment of its Fleetcare division, providing fleet management and maintenance services 'in the field' to customers across the UK. This work being undertaken both at customer sites and a number of mobile unmanned locations. The business was further consolidated with the delivery of RFS-built 90-tonne aggregate hoppers to RMC in 1990-1991 with an after market maintenance contract. A regular customer of Fleetcare services has been Redland (now Lafarge) Aggregates operating out of Mountsorrell quarry in Leicestershire, where regular preventative maintenance and annual 'VIBT' inspections are carried out on 51 ton 2-axle 'PGA' wagons and Lafarge's Self Discharge Train. Today Wabtec Rail's Fleetcare division manages the maintenance of over 2000 customer's wagons, operating in a variety of industry sectors such as aggregates, cement, petrochemical, waste disposal and rail infrastructure maintenance. More recently this has included new fleets of radio-controlled Side Tippers and High Output Ballast System (HOBS) vehicles operated by Network Rail's National Logistics Unit.

Prototype B5000 Bogies – RFS were responsible for the design and development of a number of new passenger bogie types through its Special Rail Products (SRP) division. This included the design and manufacture of suburban passenger bogies for Class 323 and 465 EMUs. Amongst SRP's more revolutionary designs was the B5000 bogie, with axle bearings mounted inboard of the wheels, dispensing with the need for stub axle ends and resulting in a significant saving on wheel and bogie frame weight. The SRP division rented industrial unit space in Hexthorpe for its bogie manufacture, but for the prototype B5000 bogies assembly was undertaken at the southern end of D Shop at Doncaster Works. The B5000 design was sold to Bombardier during RFS' receivership in 1994.

Tilcon 150 tonne Locomotive – During 1993 and 1994 RFS undertook the construction of a 150 tonne shunting locomotives for Tilcon to operate in their Swinden Quarry near Cracoe, Grassington in the Yorkshire Dales. The heaviest locomotive of its type in the UK, powered by a 375 kW Caterpillar engine and transmission and Newbrook Engineering final drive, it was designed to provide significant tractive effort to work at low speed in the steeply graded quarry conditions. Construction work took place across RFS' period of receivership, but the locomotive was successfully completed and delivered to the customer in 1994. Manufacture was undertaken in the far end of the left hand bay of the New Erecting Shop, including sub-arc welding of the massive slab underframe and buffer beams up to 12 inches thick. These operations were separately partitioned from the other work in the Shop which at that time was principally concerned with the overhaul and refurbishment of LUL C Stock. The locomotive was transported by road in three parts and assembled at the customer's site using large road cranes.

Portal Hegenscheidt Wheel Lathe – A significant portion of RFS(E)'s wheel business includes the removal and replacement of wheels worn to their minimum diameter. However there is a regular workload of wheel turning ('reprofiling') where there is sufficient thickness of material at the wheel rim not to require complete wheel replacement. Most reprofiling is undertaken on either of two Hegenscheidt wheel lathes, the largest of which is a massive 'portal' frame type shown in the photograph. This lathe originally from Shildon Wagon Works in County Durham was removed in 1983, refurbished and installed in the Heavy Shop at Doncaster Works in the summer of 1984 when the former Works was closed.

GNER Class 08 – Doncaster Works has maintained an involvement in the overhaul and repair of Class 08 shunting locomotives for many years. The privatisation of British Rail from 1994 opened up new opportunities in the shunting locomotive market for both overhaul and locomotive hire. One such case was for train operator GNER with Class 08 shunters at its maintenance depots at Bounds Green (North London) and Edinburgh Craigentinny. In 1997 RFS(E) undertook the repair and rationalisation of the existing GNER shunter fleet, entering into a hire agreement to supply a pair of shunters to each of the two depots including maintenance and repair services. Newly repainted in GNER livery shunter 08 331 (awaiting renumbering as H001) stands outside the north end of the Heavy Shop in early 1997.

Tyre Fitting – The vast majority of modern wheelsets now overhauled by RFS are of the one-piece monobloc type. However, older types of locomotive, carriage and wagon wheels, including most shunters have a separate outer rim or 'tyre' which is a shrink fit upon an inner centre. The removal and refitting of tyres on wheel centres is undertaken in a gas-fired hearth which can be expanded in size to deal with large diameter wheelsets such as is found on steam locomotive driving wheels. The wheelset is held vertically by crane and the tyre is heated by a number of gas heaters positioned around the wheel circumference. As the tyre expands the wheel centre can be either fitting into or removed from the tyre. In this view Brian Reay oversees the removal of a Class 08 tyre from its wheel centre.

Crank Axle Quartering Machine – Many shunting locomotives, such as the Class 08, and before that steam locomotives, are fitted with outside cranks to which side coupling rods are fitted. This ensures that all wheels turn at the same rate and gives a much improved adhesion between the wheel and rail. A key task in the overhaul of wheelsets fitted with outer cranks is the ability to accurately machine the crank pins relative to each other. On Class 08 shunters and 2-cylinder steam locomotives, the outer cranks are positioned at 90 degrees; on many 3-cylinder steam locomotives, the two outer cranks are at 120 degrees. The machine illustrated in the photograph is known as a quartering machine. It comprises two machining centres: one for each outer crank which can be accurately set relatively to each other to give the required distance from the centre of the axle to the centre of the crank pin (the crank throw) and the required angle between the crank pins to an accuracy of 6 minutes of arc (one tenth of a degree). From the mid-1970's a variety of wheel overhaul equipment was relocated from various parts of the Works to form a new Central Wheel Shop located in the Heavy Shop. This included machinery from both the DMU Repair Shops and the Crimpsall Wheel Alley, from where the quartering machine was originally installed. In the photograph machinist David Cassell attends to a Class 08 shunter wheelset requiring crank pin machining.

Virgin Class 90 – Early in February 1997, RFS(E) was approached by Porterbrook and Virgin Trains to relivery Class 90 electric locomotive 90002 and a Driving Van Trailer for Virgin Trains' West Coast route. Here the completed locomotive stands resplendent in the Virgin livery between the Erecting Shop and Light Shop on February 24th 1997 ready for despatch. 90002 was named Mission Impossible at a special ceremony at London Euston to launch the new Virgin Trains' West Coast franchise.

Laing Bailey Heathrow Express Construction – RFS' experience with the operation of 'Challenger' and Class 20 locomotives used in the Channel Tunnel was an important factor in the winning of further locomotive work involving tunnel operations. In September 1996 RFS(E) supplied the first of three Sentinel 0-4-0 shunters, side rod fitted No 10170, to the Laing Bailey Joint Venture company undertaking the construction of the new Heathrow Express railway. This was followed by another side rod locomotive No 10137 in November 1996 and a chain drive Sentinel No 10251 in February 1997. A fourth locomotive No D1122, an English Electric 0-4-0, followed in June 1997. All locomotives were prepared for tunnel work by adjustment of the exhaust emission levels and the fitting of catalytic converters. Locomotives were delivered to site by road and offloaded by crane, which included the delivery of early locomotives into the tunnel section by lowering into a ventilation shaft. Here RFS(E)'s Sentinel locomotives are pictured at work on the approach tracks to the tunnel section on the new railway in early 1997.

Railtrack Snowploughs – During 1997 and 1998 RFS(E) undertook a major contract to rationalise and refurbish Railtrack's fleet of 22 independent drift snowploughs. These vehicles were originally manufactured by converting withdrawn LNER 4200 gallon Group Standard 6-wheeled steam locomotive tenders in the late 1950's and early 1960's. Designed to be coupled either side of a team of locomotives, they are fitted with wooden 'dumb' buffers and are driven at speed into snowdrifts to help clear the line. The plough blades are fitted with extension pieces at the vehicle sides, which can be swung out into position when ploughing, and a rear hood to prevent snow and ice breaking the windows of the pushing locomotive. The refurbishment work included major corrosion repairs, conversion of vacuum braked ploughs to air operation and the fitting of axle roller bearings throughout. An innovative design of icicle breaker was fitted to the roof designed to hinge down if meeting an immovable object. A special intervehicle coupler was designed to permit ploughs to be moved to site coupled blade-to-blade. When not in use the coupler is lifted out of position using lifting tackle attached to the apex of the plough blade and stowed under removal plates at the front of the plough.

The upper photograph shows the extent of the vehicle bodywork repairs and the original tender underframe and suspension on snowplough ADB 965217 in the Heavy Shop in January 1998. The lower photograph from 31st March 1998 shows members of the Vehicles Division with project management staff from technical consultancy 'The engineering link' handing snowplough ADB 965232 over to Stuart Palmer (extreme right) of Railtrack.

DRS Class 20 refurbishment – 1997 saw the return of main line locomotives to the New Erecting Shop with the overhaul and refurbishment of Class 20 locomotives for Direct Rail Services (DRS) the train operating company of British Nuclear Fuels. An initial order for six Class 20's for completion by April 1998 was followed by a further order for four locomotives for October of the same year. Donor locomotives comprised former BR Telecommunications, Waterman Railways and RFS Channel Tunnel locomotives. The vehicles were stripped back to their bare frames, corroded nose ends and cabs were significantly rebuilt and the locomotives completely rewired. Part of the work included a package of modifications to bring the locomotives up to modern standards, including new headlights, cab communication equipment, and extra fuel tanks mounted on the vehicle frame and in the nose end roof space. The first two locomotives, renumbered 20306 and 20307 are pictured outside the New Erecting Shop with RFS Vehicles division personnel and support staff on 8th April 1998.

Class 59 locomotives – Between 1994 and 1995 National Power bought 6 Class 59 locomotives built by General Motors of London, Ontario in Canada, and operated a fleet of high capacity hopper wagons, including the movement of limestone from Peak Forest to Drax Power Station for desulpherisation. EWS took over the ownership and operation of the fleet and shortly after the locomotives were repainted by RFS (E) from the original blue, red, white and grey of National Power into EWS' standard livery of red and gold. Following completion of 59203 'Vale of Pickering', John Meehan (left), Managing Director of RFS(E) presents Jim Fisk, Engineering Director of EWS Railway with Gerald Coulson's commemorative painting of Mallard's world speed record run of 3rd July 1938. The presentation is being made outside RFS(E)'s newly extended paint facility at the north end of the Works site, on 21st August 1998.

Class 60 Ultrasonic Axle Testing – RFS were responsible for the assembly and supply of wheelsets during the manufacture of Class 60 locomotives between 1989 and 1993. Like a number of modern locomotives, the axles on these wheelsets have a hollow centre to reduce the unsprung wheelset mass and the forces exerted upon the track. Part of the overhaul requirements are for the internal bore of the axle to be checked for flaws by ultrasonic probe. This is achieved using a special piece of equipment which scans the inside bore of the axle and produces a computer readout highlighting any suspect areas. Here Wheel Shop Supervisor Mick Welch adjusts the set up of the equipment prior to testing a Class 60 wheelset on 9th July 2002 in No 3 Bay of D Shop (the original 1866 Tender Shop). Other hollow axle designs dealt with by Wabtec Rail include EWS Class 67 locomotives and the prototype Brush manufactured GNER Class 89 electric locomotive.

Axle Bearing Inspection – During wheelset overhaul, the axle end bearings are removed in a press, cleaned and washed of all old grease before they are given a thorough visual examination to determine whether they are fit for reuse or are to be scrapped. All manner of bearings are inspected, including spherical, cylindrical and taper roller types, including imperial and metric sizes. One of the largest bearings examined are those fitted to EuroShuttle locomotive wheels that run through the Channel Tunnel. In this photograph taken in 9th July 2002 Dave Garnham and Dennis Panks undertake bearing inspection and measurement in Wabtec Rail's Bearing House. This area is built in the east end of D5 bay, where 100 years before (as the Erecting Shop) locomotives would have entered the Works on a steam traverser.

Wabtec Rail

Railtrack High Output Ballast System Wagon manufacture – During 2001 Wabtec Rail undertook the manufacture of 190 High Output Ballast System (HOBS) vehicles for Railtrack. Based on an idea originated in late 1995 in conjunction with Tiphook Rail (now GE Capital), the HOBS vehicle is the latest generation of radio-controlled 90 tonne ballast discharge hoppers. Initially Wabtec Rail supplied 104 conversions of existing GE Capital 90-tonne hoppers to this design, most of which were undertaken during 1999 and 2000. Normally operated in sets of 10 vehicles, giving a capacity of up to 650 tonnes of aggregate, the vehicles can accurately deposit ballast in between or to either side of the track. This is achieved through the radio control of ballast discharge doors (or 'gates') beneath the vehicle body, all under the control of two operators. This gives a significant productivity improvement over conventional ballast hopper wagons.

In the upper photograph EWS Class 66 No 66100 hauls a converted 90-tonne variety of ballast hopper in the Works Yard of Wabtec Rail during a press launch on 20th April 2001. The vehicle is fitted with a diesel-alternator providing distributed electrical power for a set of 5 vehicles. The operator holds the radio-control handset and has just commenced opening of one of the discharge 'gates' from where ballast is being deposited onto the track.

Main HOBS vehicle assembly takes place in the Heavy Shop, with the installation of auxiliary systems in the Light Shop. In the lower photograph taken in the Light Shop on 18th January 2002 are vehicles stood in the assembly lines for electrical, pneumatic and hydraulic system installation. In the foreground are the 'track friendly' Axle Motion 3 bogies fitted to the HOBS vehicles. Wabtec Rail will be manufacturing a further 50 new HOBS vehicles during the summer of 2003.

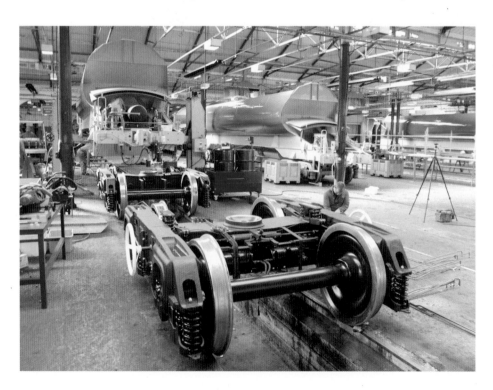

Data Recorders – Within the family of companies in the Wabtec Corporation is that of Q-Tron, based in Calgary, Canada, designers and manufacturers of data recorders (OTMRs). These devices function in a similar way to black box recorders on aircraft, by recording and storing key safety data as to how the driver is controlling the locomotive and how the vehicle is responding to those controls. This data can then be downloaded electronically for storage or analysis, and is a powerful aid in driver management. In the event of incident or accident the recorder can provide valuable data to assist in the investigation process. The recorder is constructed to give an enhanced degree of crash integrity and fire protection, and the latest versions are coloured orange to aid retrieval in a major collision or derailment. Wabtec data recorders are factory fitted to Class 66 & 67 locomotives, and have been retrofitted to a number of earlier EWS locomotives including Class 56, 58 & 60. Wabtec Rail are currently supplying over 1100 data recorders for retro fitting to Angel Trains' HST, EMU and DMU vehicles. A new Electronics Repair Centre has been established in Wabtec Rail's component overhaul facilities at Doncaster Works. Here Martin Smith tests a locomotive speedometer in Wabtec Rail's Electronic Repair Centre on 9th July 2002.

Wheel Drop Rig – Railway wheels are fitted to axles by heating in a gas oven, thereby expanding the wheel and the hole in the centre, before being accurately positioned on the axle. When it comes to removing fully worn wheels from axles, a process of oil injection is used. The wheelset is hung vertically from a crane with a large dead weight attached to the lower wheel. Hydraulic oil is pumped at very high pressure through a special drilling in the wheel centre boss, into a gallery which is machined into the inside bore of the wheel. The force of the oil overcomes the frictional forces holding the wheel onto the axle and under the action of the weight the wheel drops vertically from the axle. The wheelset is then inverted and the same process takes place for the second wheel. Oil injection is useful in that it protects the axle (often the most expensive part of the wheelset) from damage during wheel removal. Mike Hannon (left) and Geoff Griffin undertake a locomotive wheel drop in No 4 bay of D Shop on 9th July 2002.

Wabtec Rail

HAA-MHA Rebody – Wabtec Rail undertake a wide range of freight vehicle conversions but the most numerous has been that involving HAA-type coal wagons for EWS Railway. Since 1997 the company has undertaken more than 550 such conversions which involves the removal of the hopper body and bottom discharge doors by oxy-fuel cutting torch as seen in the upper photograph taken in the Works yard to the north of the Light Shop on 9th October 2002. The frames are then dressed flush and straightened of any distortion and the suspension overhauled ready to accept a new box body. The new bodies are fabricated in the Heavy Shop comprising floor plate, sides and ends and finish welded in a manipulator before final assembly to the vehicle. The converted vehicles are redesignated MHA (bottom photograph) for use on general infrastructure work.

Wabtec Rail

Passenger Bogie Overhaul – From 1998 RFS(E) and Wabtec Rail has established a significant passenger bogie overhaul business at Doncaster. With access to the national 'float' of spare bogies held by competing companies in the bogie business, RFS(E) set about creating their own float of wheelsets and components and established an industry benchmark 48-hour door to door delivery service. A franchise-length contract was won with Central Trains' Tyseley Depot (now Maintrain) to undertake C4 overhauls on Class 150 - 158 bogies. This was soon followed by the first overhauls on Class 323 EMU bogies, a bogie that had been originally designed and manufactured by the pre-receivership RFS Special Rail Products. Further success followed with a contract to undertake the first overhauls on EWS' Class 325 Royal Mail Postal EMUs. In 2001 Wabtec Rail 'stretched' a pair of Mark 3 BT10 bogies, by modifying the bogie frames and fitting longer axles to fit under an Irish Rail Snack Car (track gauge 5' 3"). Wabtec Rail now supplies a wide range of 'second generation' DMU bogies to a number of customers, including Railpart.

Top photo – In 2002 Wabtec Rail has been encouraged by its customers to venture into new bogie opportunities. Recent work has included work on Siemens Class 332 Heathrow Express and Class 333 Arriva Trains Northern EMU bogies with associated wheel work. Here John Hopkinson attends to a powered wheelset, complete with traction motor and gearbox, from a Heathrow Express EMU power bogie on 9th October 2002 in 12/13 road of the Heavy Shop.

Bottom photo – More recently Wabtec Rail has commenced a programme of Class 170 'Turbostar' C4 bogie overhauls for Maintrain on behalf of train operator Central Trains. On 13th March 2003 Brian Pinder completes a final inspection on a pair of power car bogies before despatch to the customer.

Wabtec Rail

Class 158 C6 Overhaul – Wabtec Rail has established a regular programme of passenger vehicle overhaul work including Class 156 and Class 158 DMUs. Comprising mostly of C6 overhauls, this includes dealing with corroded bodywork areas including the removal and resealing of window units, replacement of worn or damaged carpets, seats and tables and a full body and roof repaint. Customers include both Porterbrook Leasing and Angel Trains owned vehicles operated by Wessex Trains, Wales & Borders, Central Trains, Northern Spirit (now Arriva Trains Northern), First North Western and Virgin Trains. Here Angel Trains owned Class 158 DMU No 158831 for train operator Wales & Borders nears completion of its C6 overhaul and repaint in the Light Shop (former Carriage Paint Shop of 1873) on 18th January 2002.

Wheel Removal by Press – In addition to the wheel removal by oil injection, Wabtec Rail has a large capacity Hoesch MFD hydraulic press used for the removal of some types of wheel or where a wheel may have failed to be removed in the Wheel Drop Rigs. The wheel is supported at one end by crane and at the other by a rest, whilst a hydraulic ram (to the left) applies force to the axle end. This force is reacted through the wheel onto a supporting yoke manoeuvred into position behind the wheel. Removal is assisted by applying oil injection through the hose shown connected to the wheel boss. Gerry Doherty operates the Hoesch Press in D5 bay to remove a disc-braked freight wheelset in July 2002.

First Great Western Class 08 – Wabtec Rail has for many years maintained a regular programme of shunter overhaul and repair based in the New Erecting Shop. This has also included the fitting of radio control equipment enabling the locomotive to be driven from ground level by a hand held remote control handset. During 2001-2002 Wabtec Rail undertook the overhaul of nine Class 08 shunters for train operator First Great Western. On 29th April 2001 Wabtec Rail liveried Class 08 shunter No 08669 stands ready for road collection outside the west end of D2 (left) & D1 bays. Now Wabtec Rail's Wheel Shop, these two buildings were part of the original 1853 Boiler Shop (D2) and its 1866 extension (D1).

The Plant Today – This aerial shot of Doncaster Works shows how much of The Plant site exists today. The Wabtec Rail facility is predominantly contained in the large mass of buildings immediately behind Denison House (fronting the station). To the right of the picture by the River Don are some of Rail part's Main Warehouses. The large shop in the central distance is the Crimpsall, now part of Bombardier Transportation.

Wabtec Rail

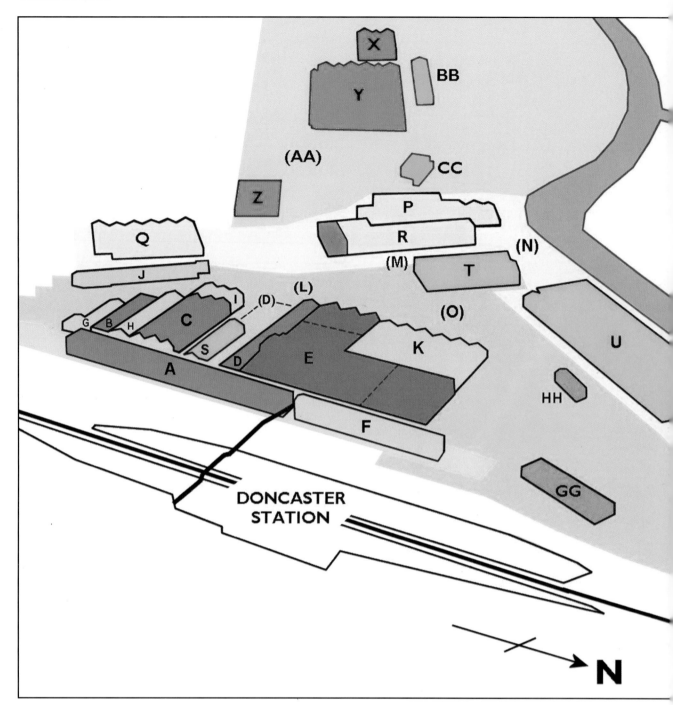

Doncaster Works Site Legend
Compare with aerial photograph of The Plant today (see page 135)

Wabtec Rail Site

Railpart Site

Bombardier Site

In Private Ownership

A 1853 Locomotive Engineer's Offices, Baths, Boiler & Engine Rooms, Upper & Lower Turneries, Carriage Shop (north end). 1935 LNER Central Drawing Offices, then BR. Now offices (Railpart & others).

B 1853 Boiler Shop (including Coppersmiths & Brass Foundry, relocated 1866). From 1882 Tender Shop. c1930 Main Machine 'D' Shop. Later Works Maintenance (1970's) then Manufacturing (1980's). 1996 Wheel Shop.

C 1853 Engine Repair Shop (30 bays with central steam traverser). 1867 Erecting Shop. c1910 vehicle frames. c1930 Main Machine 'D' Shop then Manufacturing (1980's). 1996 Wheel Shop. Birthplace of Stirling Single No 1 (1870).

D 1853/1854 Smith Shop (first Shop to open). S wing included Coppersmiths & Painters, later Millwrights & Metalling Shop. S & W wings demolished 1965. Later incorporated

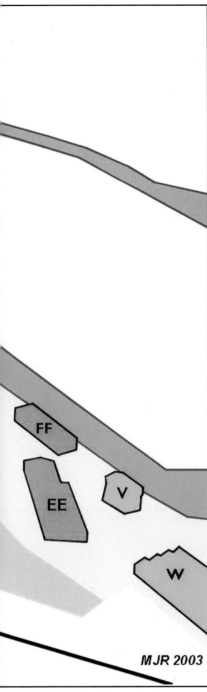

MJR 2003

J   1866 Brass Foundry & Carpenters Shop. Later Works Maintenance.

K   c1873 Carriage Paint Shop. 1965 Wagon Light Repair Shop. NowLight Shop, includes passenger vehicle overhaul work.

L   Site of 1866 Spring & Hooping Shop - demolished 1965.

M   Site of 1866 Forge (Steam Hammer Shop) - demolished 1965. Later Central Power House - demolished 1987 for access road to National Supply Centre (Railpart).

N   Site of 1866 Gas Works (extended 1881) - now Loading Bay (Railpart).

O   Site of Timber Storage & Drying Sheds - now demolished.

P   1881 Iron Foundry & Pattern Shop. 1960's Crane & Chain (including light fabrication and hay baler manufacture) Shop. Now Railpart store.

Q   1882 Stores (5 & 8 Stores). Now Railpart warehousing.

R   1882 New Boiler Shop. South end roof raised in 1907 (blue area). 1960's Fabrication Shop, including manufacture of ac electrics and Class 56 bodyshells. Now Railpart Repairables Store.

S   1891 Light Machine (B1) Shop - 1964 converted to Apprentice Training School. 1985 Components Overhaul Shop. Now Wabtec Rail Training Centre.

T   1891 New Erecting (E2) Shop. Main locomotive manufacture & assembly shop. Birthplace of Ivatt Atlantics, Flying Scotsman, Mallard, Blue Peter, Classes 03, 08, 71, 85, 86, 56 & 58. Also used for some tender construction and major fabrication work. Today used for main line locomotive and shunter overhaul & repair.

U   1890/1 West Carriage Shop. Main carriage repair shop, roof raised 1901 to install cranes in SW bays. 1960's DMU Repair Shop. Converted 1986/7 to Main Warehouse (Railpart).

V   1890/1 Tank House (including Works Water Tower).

W   1890/1 North Carriage Shed, including varnishing and light coachwork. Later included a Brass Shop, chrome plating and in 1960's DMU painting. Converted 1987 to Railpart Store.

X   1900 New Tender Shop. Tender Repair & Overhaul. 1930s Stripping Shop (boiler & superheater repairs). 1960s Locomotive Dismantling Shop. Then as Y below.

Y   1901 Crimpsall Repair Shop. Main locomotive repair shop, including wheel alley (W end). Reorganised 1930's to include tender repairs (No 1 bay). 1987 BRML Level 5 Depot, now Bombardier Transportation.

Z   1902 Locomotive Paint Shop, including 1936 Central Compressor Station. Location for Cuneo's 'Giants Refreshed'. 1987 BRML Store.

AA   Site of 1935 Locomotive Weigh House. Dismantled 1997.

BB   1960's Diesel Store, later Power Unit Shop (1970's), Central Store and Paint Shop (1990's).

CC   1965 Locomotive Test House.

DD   1960's DMU Test House & Asbestos Shop. From 1987 Railpart Store.

EE   Railpart Flammable Store.

FF   Railpart Glass Store.

GG   Wet Blast Facility (1988) converted to Paint Shop (1994) extended 1998.

HH   Vehicle Shot Blast Facility.

Joiners/Sawmill & Damper Shop (from 1987). 2001 Refurbished as Component Shop

E   Site of 1853 Carriage & Wagon Shops (shown dotted). Extended 1866 & 1873. From 1889 Main Carriage Shop, including manufacture of 1930's Silver Jubilee & Coronation carriages. December 1940 destroyed by accidental fire. 1947-9 rebuilt as Carriage Shop (with Trimming Shop E side). 1965 Wagon Heavy Repair Shop. 1975 onwards incorporated Central Wheel Shop at south end. 1996 former Trimming Shop converted to Wabtec Rail Offices. 1998 12/13 roads Bogie Overhaul Bay.

F   1866 Carriage Trimming Shop (south end built over (1853 Weigh House). 1941 CME's Offices. Now office accommodation (EWS & others).

G   1866 Extension to Boiler Shop. From 1882 Tender Shop. Then as B above.

H   1866 Tender Shop. c1910 Carriage underframes. Then as C above.

I   1866 extension to Erecting Shop (further 12 bays).

Wabtec Rail

Sprinter Gearbox Overhaul – From the earliest days of the introduction of the Class 150 type 'Sprinters' in the mid-1980's the Works has developed and maintained an expertise in the overhaul of Gmeinder gearboxes fitted to these DMU's. These 'right-angle' drive units transmit the drive from the underbody-mounted diesel engine and gearbox through ninety degrees to drive the axles. On Sprinter type units one bogie is powered, the other is a non-powered trailer. On the powered bogie there are two final drives; a 'master' which receives the input from the body-mounted transmission and a 'slave' which is driven from the 'master'. Wabtec Rail's gearbox cell is located in D4 bay of the Wheel Shop and overhauls DMU and Class 323 EMU gearboxes. Here Chris Dibb measures the backlash in the bevel gears between the crown wheel (the large gear on the axle) and the pinion on 9th July 2002.

Network Rail New Measurement Train – In 2003 Wabtec Rail has undertaken conversion work for Serco Railtest for the Network Rail New Measurement Train (NMT). Comprising three converted Mark 3 trailer vehicles and two Mark 2 test vehicles between Class 43 High Speed Train Power Cars, the NMT will travel the UK rail network collecting key infrastructure data enroute. Wabtec Rail have principally been involved in the conversion of one of the Mark 2 test vehicles, DB 995550, the High Speed Track Recording Coach in addition to other modification work on the Power Cars. One of the three HST Power Cars undergoes modification to its nose end in the Light Shop on 28th March 2003.